Judge Advocates in Vietnam: Army Lawyers in Southeast Asia 1959-1975

by
Frederic L. Borch III

U.S. Army Command and General Staff College Press
Fort Leavenworth, Kansas 66027-6900

COMBAT
STUDIES
INSTITUTE

Contents

Foreword

Although the first American soldiers arrived in Saigon in late 1950, the first Army judge advocate did not deploy to Vietnam until 1959, when Lt. Col. Paul J. Durbin reported for duty. From then until 1975 when Saigon fell and the last few U.S. military personnel left Vietnam, Army lawyers played a significant role in what is still America's "longest war."

Judge Advocates in Vietnam: Army Lawyers in Southeast Asia (1959-1975) tells the story of these soldier-lawyers in headquarters units like the Saigon-based Military Assistance Advisory Group and Military Assistance Command, Vietnam (MACV). But it also examines the individual experiences of judge advocates in combat organizations like II Field Force, 1ˢᵗ Air Cavalry Division, and the 25ᵗʰ Infantry Division. Almost without exception, Army lawyers recognized that the unconventional nature of guerrilla warfare required them to practice law in new and non-traditional ways. Consequently, many judge advocates serving in Vietnam between 1959 and 1975 looked for new ways to use their talent and abilities—both legal and non-legal—to enhance mission success. While this was not what judge advocates today refer to as "operational law"—that compendium of domestic, foreign, and international law applicable to U.S. forces engaged in combat or operations other than war—the efforts of these Vietnam-era lawyers were a major force in shaping today's view that judge advocates are most effective if they are integrated into Army operations at all levels.

Judge Advocates in Vietnam is not the first book about lawyering in Southeast Asia. On the contrary, Maj. Gen. George S. Prugh's *Law at War*, published in 1975, was the first look at what judge advocates did in Vietnam. General Prugh's monograph, however, focuses exclusively on legal work done at MACV. Similarly, Col. Fred Borch's *Judge Advocates in Combat: Army Lawyers in Military Operations from Vietnam to Haiti* has a chapter on law in Southeast Asia, but it is a very brief look at military lawyering in Vietnam. It follows that this new Combat Studies Institute publication is long overdue. Its comprehensive examination of judge advocates in Vietnam—who was there, what they did, and how they did it—fills a void in the history of the Army and the Judge Advocate General's Corps. At the same time, anyone who takes the time to read these pages will come away with a greater appreciation of what it was like to serve as a soldier—and an Army lawyer—in Vietnam.

Thomas J. Romig
Major General, U.S. Army
The Judge Advocate General

v

Introduction

This is a narrative history of Army lawyers in Vietnam from 1959—when the first judge advocate reported for duty in Vietnam—to 1975—when the last Army lawyer left Saigon.

Its principal theme is that, as the Army developed new strategies and tactics to combat the guerilla war waged by the Viet Cong and North Vietnamese, Army judge advocates also discovered that the unconventional nature of the war required them to find new ways of using the law, and their skills as lawyers, to enhance mission success.

When people read about those who served as soldier-lawyers in Southeast Asia from 1959 to 1975, they want answers to at least three questions: Who was there? What did they do? How did that enhance the commanders' ability to accomplish the assigned mission?

In answering the first two questions, *Judge Advocates in Vietnam* identifies the men and women who deployed to Southeast Asia; it looks at selected courts-martial, military personnel and foreign claims, legal assistance, administrative and contract law issues, and international law matters handled by those judge advocates. Examining who was there and what they did is important because it captures for posterity the contribution of judge advocates of an earlier era. Viewed from this perspective, *Judge Advocates in Vietnam* is a contemporary branch history. However, in light of its principal theme, *Judge Advocates in Vietnam* answers the third question by focusing on those events where Army lawyers used the law and lawyering in non-traditional ways.

As in World War II and the Korean War, the mainstay of lawyering for Vietnam-era members of the Judge Advocate General's Corps continued to be military justice, legal assistance, claims, and administrative, civil and international law. While judge advocates in previous armed conflicts had practiced law away from the battlefield, Vietnam required Army lawyers to take their practice from the "rear" to the "front," going to those areas where American soldiers were in imminent contact with the enemy. To some extent, the guerilla tactics used by the Viet Cong meant that the "battlefield" was everywhere, but the increased operational tempo of the U.S. Army also meant that effective lawyering could not be done too far from the frontlines. For example, the airmobility of the 1st Cavalry Division caused its judge advocates to conduct legal operations in new ways. With about 450 helicopters, the division was not dependent upon ground transportation for movement, either tactically or administratively. This meant that 1st

Cavalry had a very large area of operations and that its firebases were located a great distances from its headquarters. In 1970, with all lawyers located at the division main headquarters at Phuoc Vin, activities such as interviewing witnesses for trial, advising convening authorities located outside of Phuoc Vin and, in some instances, actively conducting courts-martial at firebases, required travelling by air. Additionally, troops normally did not come into headquarters for personal legal assistance or to file claims; judge advocates took legal services to them. Even Lt. Col. Ronald M. Holdaway, the division Staff Judge Advocate, was routinely airborne as he left the rear and flew to base camps and firebases to confer with and advise commanders. As a principal staff officer, Holdaway was normally able to obtain a helicopter for all of his missions. Thanks to the division chief of staff, Col. (later General) Edward C. Meyer, lawyers who worked for Holdaway obtained helicopter support for most of their legal work, too.

While Colonel Holdaway and his judge advocates proved that Army lawyers could—and did—take their legal operations to the field, members of the Corps also used the law and their training as attorneys to blaze new paths, enhancing mission success in nontraditional ways. Lawyers who took on nontraditional roles did so on an individual basis; there was no institutional recognition that such matters were appropriate issues for judge advocates. In 1960, for example, during a coup d'etat led by disaffected South Vietnamese paratroopers, Army judge advocate Lt. Col. Paul J. Durbin left the safety of his home to observe the rebels in action. As a result, Durbin was able to see—and explain—to an American adviser accompanying the coup leader that "advising" this Vietnamese paratroop colonel did not include participating in a rebellion against the Saigon government. Lt. Col. George C. Eblen, who followed Durbin as the lone Army judge advocate in Vietnam, decided to begin monitoring war crimes committed by the Viet Cong against Americans. Eblen's decision to tape record all interviews of U.S. personnel claiming mistreatment resulted in a command policy that a military lawyer participate in all future debriefings involving war crimes. Again, like Durbin, Colonel Eblen stepped outside his traditional role.

Similarly, Col. (later Maj. Gen.) George S. Prugh, staff judge advocate for the Military Assistance Command, Vietnam (MACV) from 1964 to 1966, spearheaded a number of unique efforts: creating the U.S.-Vietnamese Law Society and arranging for Vietnamese lawyers to study in the United States, compiling and translating all existing Vietnamese laws and establishing a legal advisory program that monitored the real-world operation of South Vietnam's criminal justice system.

Of particular significance was Colonel Prugh's successful effort in persuading the South Vietnamese military that its conflict with the Viet Cong and North Vietnamese was no longer an internal civil disorder. This was a significant achievement in that once its military leaders had accepted the international nature of the conflict, the South Vietnamese government also acceded to this view and agreed that the provisions of the 1949 Geneva Convention on Prisoners of War would be applied.

Persuading the South Vietnamese armed forces to change their position concerning the conflict and therefore their view of the status and treatment of Viet Cong and North Vietnamese prisoners was not a judge advocate responsibility, and Colonel Prugh had not been tasked with resolving this matter. Recognizing, however, that the increasing number of Americans captured by the Viet Cong and North Vietnamese would have significantly enhanced chances to survive if South Vietnam applied the Geneva Prisoners of War Convention to enemy soldiers in its custody, Prugh and his staff spearheaded the efforts to bring about this change.

After Prugh's departure from Vietnam, his successor Col. Edward W. Haughney continued using the law to support the mission in related ways. Thus, while the MACV provost marshal was primarily responsible for advising the Vietnamese on prisoner of war issues, Haughney and his staff promulgated the first procedural framework for classifying combat captives, using so-called Article 5 tribunals. They also took the initiative in establishing a records system identifying and listing all prisoners of war.

The individual initiatives of Colonels Durbin, Eblen, Prugh, and Haughney illustrated how judge advocates could provide support on a broad range of legal and nonlegal issues associated with operations at the Military Assistance Advisory Group and the Military Assistance Command, Vietnam. Their efforts also demonstrated that Army lawyers could properly focus on more than the traditional peacetime issues of military justice, claims, administrative law, and legal assistance.

The story of judge advocates in Vietnam is a rich and varied one, and demonstrates that Army lawyers were adept at handling more than traditional legal missions, and could enhance the success of military operations in a variety of non-traditional ways. This book offers some interpretations about the role played by Army lawyers in Southeast

Asia. Ultimately, however, conclusions about the impact of judge advocates on the Army's Vietnam experience are best left to each reader.

Fred L. Borch
Colonel, Judge Advocate General's Corps
August 2003
The Pentagon, Washington, D.C.

Chapter 1

Vietnam: Judge Advocates in the Early Years 1959–1965

"Will you go to Vietnam?" I was asked in late 1958.
I said: "Where is that? And what will I do?"[1]

—Col. Paul J. Durbin
First judge advocate in Vietnam

Background

American involvement in Vietnam began at the end of World War II. Believing that Ho Chi Minh and the Viet Minh would set up a Communist state if the French were ousted from Indochina, the United States went to the active aid of the French. For the next thirty years, Vietnam was the centerpiece of U.S. containment policy in Southeast Asia and the battleground for America's longest war. Before American involvement ended in 1975, some 3.5 million members of the Army, Navy, Air Force, Marine Corps, and Coast Guard would serve in Vietnam and roughly 58,000 would lose their lives there.

The U.S. Army's presence in Vietnam began in August 1950, when President Harry S. Truman established the U.S. Military Assistance Advisory Group (MAAG), Indochina. Initially, the advisory group funneled American equipment to the French and advised only on the use of that materiel. With the departure of the French and the creation of the Republic of Vietnam in 1955, however, American soldiers assigned to the renamed Military Assistance Advisory Group, Vietnam, began advising South Vietnamese Army units on tactics, training, and logistics—any matter that would improve combat effectiveness.

By mid-1960 the advisory group numbered nearly 700 U.S. Army, Navy, Air Force, and Marine Corps personnel, all of whom advised their counterparts in the roughly 150,000-man Republic of Vietnam Armed Forces. The Army of the Republic of Vietnam, with a strength of about 140,000, made up the bulk of the South Vietnamese military; U.S. Army personnel were the largest advisory component, and the chief of the MAAG was a senior Army general officer.

The task of the South Vietnamese Army was to maintain "internal security" and resist "external attack."[2] This meant combating the growing Communist-led guerrilla insurgency, or Viet Cong, and delaying any North Vietnamese invasion until the arrival of American reinforcements. Consequently, advisers reorganized the South Vietnamese Army into standard infantry divisions, compatible in design with this two-part military mission. In time, the advisers busied themselves with every aspect of the South Vietnamese Army, from administrative procedures, personnel management, logistics, and intelligence to unit training, mobilization, war planning, and leadership.[3]

After President John F. Kennedy took office in January 1961, the United States took an increasingly aggressive role in South Vietnam. Kennedy sent U.S. Army Special Forces teams and helicopters to Vietnam. Advisers, who previously had been placed at the division level, were now permanently assigned to infantry battalions and certain lower echelon combat units.[4] In February 1962, the Joint Chiefs of Staff created the United States Military Assistance Command, Vietnam (MACV), as the senior American military headquarters in Vietnam. U.S. forces had increased to 11,000 men, and the MACV commander, a four-star Army general, worked diligently to combat the growing strength of the guerrillas who, aided by the North Vietnamese, were everywhere undermining the government of President Ngo Dinh Diem. Although the advisory group was not formally dissolved until May 1964, the Saigon-based MACV now directed the ever-expanding American involvement in that country.

Judge Advocate Operations at the Military Assistance Advisory Group, Vietnam

The mission of the staff judge advocate in the MAAG was to render legal aid and advice to the members of the advisory element and to act as legal adviser to the Director of Military Justice, the Judge Advocate General equivalent in the South Vietnamese armed forces.[5] In regards to advising the Vietnamese, the American view was that the legal adviser's chief duty was to evaluate the effectiveness of the Vietnamese military justice system and to transform it from a French-based paper structure to a workable U.S.-style system akin to the Uniform Code of Military Justice.[6] Finally, as the U.S. embassy in Saigon did not have a lawyer among its personnel, the MAAG staff judge advocate provided legal advice to the ambassador and his staff.

Lt. Col. Paul J. Durbin was the first military lawyer assigned for duty in Vietnam. He was an ideal choice for a legal adviser. As a former infantry officer with World War II combat experience, Durbin had an immediate rapport with the two MAAG commanders for whom he worked from 1959 to 1961, Army Lt. Gen. Samuel T. Williams and Army Lt. Gen. Lionel C. McGarr. Durbin also was a seasoned military lawyer. After becoming a judge advocate in 1948, he had served as a lawyer in Japan and in Korea, having gone ashore as a judge advocate in the amphibious landing at Inchon in 1950. Durbin had also been the staff judge advocate for the 7th Infantry Division, 1st and 4th Armored Divisions, and 82d and 101st Airborne Divisions. No military lawyer had more experience with troops than Durbin, and this, combined with his judge advocate background, meant he was well prepared to be the first military lawyer in Vietnam.[7]

After attending a four-week orientation course for MAAG personnel in Washington, D.C., Lt. Col. Durbin took a Pan American flight to Vietnam in June 1959. Almost all the 700 or so members of the advisory group lived in hotels during their year-long assignment. Durbin, however, was one of the approximately forty members of the element on an accompanied two-year tour, so his wife, daughter, and son arrived in country about six weeks later. The Durbins lived in a house in Saigon, where life generally was good and relatively safe.

Lt. Col. Durbin was a one-man legal operation. Other than a part-time Vietnamese secretary assisting with typing, he had no staff. He was on his own in Vietnam.[8] Moreover, Durbin got little guidance from the Judge Advocate General's Office, or "JAGO" as it was known. This was not only because communication was difficult (it was not possible to pick up the telephone and place a call to Washington, D.C.), but also because judge advocates in those days were not accustomed to ask for technical assistance from the Pentagon, much less coordinate with it on a routine basis. Nevertheless, Durbin did have visitors from Washington at least once a year by virtue of Article 6, Uniform Code of Military Justice, which required frequent inspections of staff

Lt. Col. Paul J. Durbin, shown here as a colonel, was the first military lawyer in Vietnam. Durbin served as the MAAG staff judge advocate from June 1959 to July 1961. He returned to Vietnam for a second time in 1966, when he served first as II Field Force staff judge advocate and then as a military judge with the Army Trial Judiciary.

judge advocate operations in the field by the Judge Advocate General or senior members of his staff.

Lt. Col. Durbin served in Vietnam until August 1961. He was replaced by Lt. Col. George C. Eblen, who arrived that same month. Born in France of an American father and a French mother, Eblen spoke fluent French, and so was well-suited to liaison with Vietnamese government officials, many of whom were French-educated and spoke better French than English. Complementing his language skills was his superb background as an officer and attorney. A former World War II infantry officer who fought with the 12th Armored Division in France and Germany, Eblen left active duty at the end of the war and finished law school in 1949. He then requested a return to active duty with the Judge Advocate General's Department. After some training at the Pentagon, Eblen served overseas in both France and Germany. He subsequently served at Fort Knox, Kentucky, and in the Pentagon. In short, Eblen arrived in Vietnam a well-rounded and experienced Army lawyer.

Col. Paul J. Durbin and the author, Honolulu, Hawaii, December 2001. After retiring in 1968, Durbin opened up a solo law practice and, although now in his mid-80s, he still appears on behalf of clients in Hawaii Family Court.

Like Durbin, Eblen found that he was a one-man legal operation. The creation of the MACV and the increasing number of Army, Navy, Air Force, and Marine Corps personnel meant more lawyers were needed. Consequently, about six months into his tour Lt. Col. Eblen was joined by an Air Force lawyer and a Navy lawyer. This assignment of two non-Army "deputies" at the MAAG staff judge advocate office continued after Eblen returned to the United States in late July 1962.[9] Additionally, his staff increased to include two Army judge advocates, 1st Lt. Thomas C. Graves, who arrived in February 1962, and Maj. Madison C. Wright, who arrived the next month. Eblen also obtained two legal clerks and a Vietnamese interpreter-secretary.

4

Legal Advice to the Military Assistance Advisory Group

In addition to being the adviser to the Directorate of Military Justice, Lt. Col. Durbin and the Army lawyers who followed him provided a full range of legal services to members of the advisory component, such as wills, powers of attorney, tax assistance, and advice on domestic relations, civil suits, and filing claims for damaged property.

Durbin and the early judge advocates also provided command advice, particularly in the area of discipline. Criminal jurisdiction over MAAG personnel was exclusively under the Uniform Code of Military Justice; the government of South Vietnam had neither criminal nor civil jurisdiction over those assigned to the advisory group. This unusual situation resulted from the Agreement for Mutual Defense Assistance in Indochina, commonly known as the Pentalateral Agreement. Negotiated in December 1950 by the United States, France, Laos, Vietnam, and Cambodia, this international agreement provided MAAG officers with diplomatic status, which carried with it complete criminal and civil immunity from Vietnamese law. Enlisted soldiers enjoyed diplomatic status equivalent to that of clerical personnel assigned to the U.S. embassy. As the Pentalateral Agreement did not describe the difference between these two types of diplomatic status, however, the practical effect was that MAAG enlisted personnel also enjoyed complete immunity from Vietnamese law. The Pentalateral Agreement also exempted all goods imported into Vietnam for use by the advisory group from Vietnamese customs and taxes. This special treatment reflected a belief that there would be only a small U.S. presence in Vietnam after 1950. As the American buildup began in the early 1960s, however, the United States and the Republic of Vietnam chose not to negotiate a status of forces agreement like those in force in Japan, Korea, and the Philippines. Consequently, all U.S. forces remained immune from Vietnamese criminal and civil law until the end of the war in 1975.

Despite this diplomatic status, MAAG regulations required U.S. personnel to respect Vietnamese law. Both governments were particularly concerned that the economy of South Vietnam not be disrupted by currency manipulation. Some Americans, however, could not resist the lure of illegally changing money for profit. In August 1960, for example, Lt. Col. Durbin reviewed an investigation of a soldier who exchanged U.S. doilars for Vietnamese piasters outside of the official banking system.[10] Although no adverse action was taken in that case, those caught illegally exchanging piasters for dollars were either administratively disciplined or given nonjudicial punishment under Article 15 of the Uniform Code or both.

The other area of criminal activity requiring judge advocate involvement was black-marketing in U.S. goods. American-made alcohol, cigarettes, and candy, for example, were very expensive in Vietnam; their tax-free purchase by MAAG troops for resale to Vietnamese nationals was thus illegal under Vietnamese law and an abuse of the diplomatic privileges granted U.S. personnel under the Pentalateral Agreement. As a result, Lt. Col. Durbin assisted in drafting a general regulation forbidding such transactions, although given the small size of the advisory group, black-marketing in U.S. goods was not a significant problem.[11]

No courts-martial were convened at the MAAG prior to Lt. Col. Durbin's arrival or during his tenure as staff judge advocate. The small size of the advisory element and the quality of people assigned to it meant that there was little crime that could not be handled under Article 15 of the Uniform Code. In these cases, Durbin advised the command and also informed the accused of his rights and options in nonjudicial proceedings.

Lt. Col. Durbin set up a claims office for Vietnamese whose property was damaged by MAAG members, mostly in traffic accidents involving military vehicles. He discovered, however, that the concept of filing a claim against the government was completely foreign to the Vietnamese; they did not make claims against their own government and so did not readily pursue claims for damages against the United States. Additionally, Durbin "found out that the fellow I'd set up in the claims office was operating on his own—he was bringing claimants in to file false claims in return for money." Durbin told this employee that his services were no longer required.[12]

A few months after settling his family in Saigon, Durbin found himself in the midst of an attempted coup d'etat against the Diem government. At 0300 on 11 November 1960, three battalions of South Vietnamese paratroopers surrounded the presidential palace. While President Diem took refuge in the palace wine cellar, the rebels demanded certain reforms, including "free elections, freedom of the press, and a more effective campaign against the Viet Cong."[13] Significantly, the MAAG chief, Lt. Gen. McGarr, and U.S. Ambassador Elbridge Durbrow attempted to remain neutral—indicating U.S. support for the rebels' demands for some social and political reform.

That morning, 11 November, Durbin awoke in the dark to the sound of automatic weapons fire. A radio station was just down the street from his quarters, and he assumed that the gunfire was the result of the rebels attempting a takeover of that station. Using the MAAG telephone system, a line of which was connected directly to his home, Lt. Col. Durbin contacted the advisory group. He learned that a coup was in progress and that he should stay put. When the firing stopped that afternoon, however, Durbin ventured out. His first choice was to drive his automobile to the MAAG compound some seven miles away but, as he was unarmed, Durbin thought he might be safer on foot. Consequently, he left his car in his driveway and started walking toward the presidential palace. Durbin saw a jeep go by him with a paratrooper colonel, one of the coup leaders. Durbin was shocked to see an American Army captain seated next to the rebel colonel. Durbin flagged down the jeep and asked the American officer what he was doing. When the captain replied that he was with the Vietnamese colonel because he was his adviser, Durbin asked rhetorically if "he was advising on the coup." Durbin then told the American officer to get out of the jeep and disappear.[14]

Although the attempted coup lasted a mere three days, the event made Lt. Col. Durbin think about legal issues that he had not anticipated when arriving in Vietnam the year before. As another coup attempt seemed likely, Durbin wanted to inform himself of the status of the advisory group and its members and the role that they should assume in the event of another coup. On 28 June 1961, after consulting with the International Law Division at the Judge Advocate General's Office in Washington and the U.S. embassy in Saigon, Durbin produced written guidance for MAAG personnel in the "event of a breakdown of internal law and order within South Vietnam," which was placed in a legal annex to MAAG Vietnam Operations Plan 61–61.[15]

Durbin's annex asked and answered four related questions: To what extent could MAAG advisers act in defense of their billets and property in a future coup? Suppose those forcing entry into those billets were loyal South Vietnamese troops seeking a "tactical advantage" for employing weapons? Or rebels looking for a better fighting position? Durbin's answer was that, as the Pentalateral Agreement gave diplomatic status to all MAAG personnel, their billets "should be considered immune from entry except with the consent of the Chief of the U.S. Diplomatic Mission." Consequently, MAAG personnel "would be legally justified" in using all force necessary to prevent such entry. Durbin cautioned, however, that whether using such force was "politically or personally wise" depended on the circumstances surrounding the event. He also advised that the diplomatic status of MAAG members meant that their billets and property should be considered "extensions of the Embassy," so that all requests for evacuation should be refused unless considered necessary for "self-preservation."[16]

The second point raised in the annex was whether MAAG billets or buildings could be used to give shelter or asylum to important civilian and military leaders during an "internal disorder." Lt. Col. Durbin wrote that in the context of a future coup d'etat, "foreign diplomats have no right under customary international law to grant asylum to any individual who takes refuge on Embassy property." Consequently, MAAG personnel lacked the authority to grant asylum to Vietnamese military and civilian officials. That said, however, Durbin advised that "temporary asylum" could be given "against the violent and disorderly action of irresponsible sections of the population" and that MAAG members could grant such temporary asylum for "compelling considerations of humanity." Durbin cautioned, however, that the right to such asylum would end when the disorder ceased.[17]

A third issue was whether MAAG personnel had the authority to restrain the South Vietnamese military detachment guarding the MAAG compound from attacking any rebel force that might pass by, particularly as such an attack by loyal forces might invite a rebel attack on the advisory group. Durbin answered that the advisory group had no authority over the detachment and could only "inform or remind the guard detachment of its duties toward Embassy personnel and property." Presumably such a reminder might dissuade the guards from attacking rebel forces.[18]

Finally, Lt. Col. Durbin addressed the legality of a Vietnamese search of official U.S. aircraft for rebels fleeing the country in the aftermath of an internal disorder. If such a search was a violation of international law, should it be resisted by U.S. personnel? Durbin wrote that the search would be unlawful, and that military aircraft enjoy, in principle, the same inviolability that foreign warships and embassy property enjoy under customary international law. As a result, local authorities could not "forcibly" remove any refugee, "even one who has committed a crime." That said, Durbin advised that there was authority for the view that "fugitive criminals" might be seized on grounds of "self-preservation."[19]

Lt. Col. Eblen and his legal staff, like Lt. Col. Durbin before them, provided legal assistance and claims advice to MAAG members. They also began investigating alleged violations of the Law of War. Some Special Forces advisers captured by the Viet Cong had escaped. Eblen interviewed them and tape recorded their allegations of mistreatment while in captivity. This judge advocate involvement resulted in a MAAG policy requiring that a military lawyer participate in any future interviews or debriefings involving alleged war crimes. By mid-1962, reports of war crimes committed by the guerrillas increased to such a level that Eblen tasked his Air Force judge advocate, Maj. Lucian M. Ferguson, with creating case files indexing allegations of mistreatment by subject matter and the identity of the perpetrator.[20] Eblen's interest in monitoring war crimes later became the basis for a MACV directive requiring the reporting and investigation of all such incidents.

In the area of military justice, Lt. Col. Eblen decided in early 1962 that the advisory group's increased size, and the related increase in criminal misconduct, made it desirable to convene summary and special courts-martial in Vietnam. Under the 1951 *Manual for Courts-Martial* then in effect, military lawyers had little involvement in these courts, providing only guidance to the line officers serving as prosecutors and defense counsel and reviewing completed summary and special courts for legal correctness. Undeterred, Eblen discussed the issue with his South Vietnamese counterpart, Col. Nguyen Van Mau, the Director of Military Justice. Eblen told him that the U.S. forces in Vietnam had certain "discipline problems" requiring "action." Col. Mau responded that as the Pentalateral Agreement did not prohibit the convening of courts-martial, he would not object, although he cautioned Eblen not to request written approval for U.S. military courts to operate in Vietnam, inferring that a formal request would be denied as an infringement of sovereignty.

Mau's tacit approval was all Eblen needed, and before long, summary and special courts-martial were being convened in Vietnam.[21] And not just in Vietnam. American forces were also in Thailand as part of a military advisory effort, and Gen. Paul D. Harkins, the MACV chief, traveled to Bangkok to discuss a possible status of forces agreement between the United States and Thailand. While in Bangkok, Harkins learned from his Thai counterpart that although the Thai government "would impose no objection to the convening of courts-martial in Thailand by U.S. authorities" and was agreeable to the United States having exclusive criminal jurisdiction over its forces, there was "a great reluctance to sign anything" to that effect. Based on his experience in Vietnam, Lt. Col. Eblen advised Gen. Harkins that convening courts-martial on the basis of the Thai government's tacit approval would establish a precedent that "would have the same effect in this part of the world as would a written document."[22]

No general courts-martial were convened in Vietnam during Lt. Col. Eblen's tenure as staff judge advocate. This was because the advisory group was not a general court-martial convening authority, and also because the command's policy was that any soldier, sailor, airman, or Marine meriting trial by general court-martial was no longer needed in Vietnam. Consequently, where a general court was appropriate, charges were preferred and an Article 32 investigation was held in Vietnam. For referral, the accused and the entire case packet were sent to Schofield Barracks in Hawaii or to Clark Air Base or Subic Bay Naval Base in the Philippines, depending on the accused's branch of service.[23]

Lt. Col. George C. Eblen, left, with Lt. Gen. Le Van Ty, Chief of Staff, Army of the Republic of Vietnam, before leaving on an inspection tour of Vietnam, 10 February 1962. Eblen was the second judge advocate to deploy to Vietnam. He retired in 1966 and died in 2001.

"Advising" the Vietnamese

Believing that South Vietnam's military justice system would work better if modeled after American rather than French military law, Lt. Col. Durbin met every Wednesday afternoon with Col. Mau to draft a new criminal code for the South Vietnamese armed forces. Durbin had the 1928 *Manual for Courts-Martial*, which he thought "ideal for the Vietnamese Army because it was much more simple than the 1951 *Manual*—not necessarily better—just simpler." The remainder of Durbin's legal library consisted of the Court-Martial Reports, the "red books" containing courts-martial cases decided on appeal by the Army Board of Review and Court of Military Appeals. He also had some Army regulations. He did not have anything else.[24]

Durbin's methodology was to go through the Uniform Code article by article, explaining military practice and procedure to his Vietnamese counterparts. Vietnamese judge advocates were receptive to most of the

Uniform Code, and Durbin worked especially hard on altering the role of the Vietnamese judge advocate in capital cases. The Viet Cong were murdering village chiefs, and, if caught, they were prosecuted in South Vietnamese military courts. The sentence was usually death, and a substantial number of executions occurred. Durbin learned that a Vietnamese armed forces lawyer presided at the imposition of every death sentence, supervising the beheading by guillotine. Believing that the carrying out of a sentence was more properly a police rather than a judicial function, Durbin told the Vietnamese judge advocates that it was inappropriate for an officer of the court to preside over an execution. Police authorities, he argued, were better suited to sentencing tasks. Durbin's work on a new Vietnamese code of military justice was never finished, and the project was abandoned after his departure in July 1961.

As Vietnam's top military lawyer, Col. Mau was not only the Director of Military Justice, but also the chief of the Gendarmerie. Consequently, Lt. Col. Durbin worked to understand the Gendarmerie and advise his colleague how to make it function better. Modeled after the French force of the same name, the Gendarmerie was a national police force that "filled a gap between military and civilian law enforcement."[25] Known as "the Red Hats" after their distinctive red berets, the Gendarmerie was a rural-based "judicial police" empowered to conduct investigations for the Vietnamese courts. The members of the Gendarmerie could apprehend both civilians and military personnel. They also could take sworn statements that were admissible in court, and so were an important part of the judicial process in addition to their law enforcement role. Additionally, the Red Hats were a respected symbol of authority and in many areas were the only contact the local population had with the Saigon government. Durbin recognized soon after his arrival that the Gendarmerie was an important organization that could benefit from American advice and support, and he worked to preserve it. The MAAG provost marshal, however, opposed the Gendarmerie and worked to prevent it from receiving MAAG funds. For example, money was made available to the Vietnamese military police to purchase handcuffs while the Gendarmerie was told to secure prisoners with rope. Viewing police functions in terms of their own experience, the provost marshal and other MAAG police advisers failed to appreciate the Gendarmerie's value, as it "did not fall into any familiar category of American law enforcement organization." Despite Durbin's protests and his recommendation that the Gendarmerie be increased rather than decreased in size, it was increasingly deprived of MAAG funding and was disbanded on 1 January 1965. In retrospect, this was a serious error, for it removed a visible government presence in the countryside and disrupted military judicial operations "for a considerable period of time."[26]

Durbin's other major advisory efforts were teaching law and English to the South Vietnamese. The courts and the legal profession played a small part in Vietnamese society, principally because Confucianism encouraged negotiation and adjustment rather than conflict. Consequently, the Vietnamese were reluctant to bring civil disputes to court, and there were remarkably few lawyers available. During Durbin's tenure as staff judge advocate, Vietnam had a population of about sixteen million, yet it had only about 160 practicing lawyers.[27] By comparison, California, with a population slightly larger than that of South Vietnam during that period, had about 25,000 practicing attorneys. All Vietnamese lawyers were graduates of the law school in either Hue or Saigon. Lt. Col. Durbin decided that his advisory efforts should begin with law students, so he contacted the University of Saigon law school soon after his arrival. A prerequisite for graduation was a law course taught in a foreign language. As a practical matter, a professor from a French law faculty traveled yearly to Saigon to teach this required course, but in 1960, no one was coming. This fact, lamented the dean of the law school to Durbin, meant the law school would have no graduates that year. Durbin quickly recommended a solution. He created a new course, "American Jurisprudence," which he taught every Saturday morning to an enthusiastic group of sixty to seventy law students. The highlight of the course was a mock jury trial modeled after an actual Kentucky criminal case familiar to Durbin from his years of private law practice in that state. The students played the roles of defendant, prosecutor, defense counsel, judge, and jury, with the proceedings held at the Palace of Justice. Durbin recognized that teaching the course would bring him into contact with the future leaders of the Vietnamese judicial establishment, yet his teaching was also a labor of love. It was a mark of the value of the class that MACV lawyers continued providing this instruction in later years as well.[28]

Durbin also taught English at the Vietnamese-American Association. The association, sponsored by the U.S. embassy, coordinated English classes and paid those teaching a small stipend in Vietnamese piasters. Teaching English brought judge advocates in contact with Vietnamese officials and so aided the advisory effort in Vietnam. Durbin taught twelve to twenty students over a twelve-month period, beginning with basic English speaking skills and ending with written composition.[29]

After Lt. Col. Durbin left Vietnam in August 1961, Lt. Col. Eblen continued a number of his advisory programs. Eblen met weekly with the Director of Military Justice. These meetings, conducted entirely in French, discussed matters of mutual interest. Eblen learned, for example, that the South Vietnamese were no longer interested in modeling their military criminal law system after the Uniform Code of Military Justice, if they ever had been. The French had imposed their system on the Vietnamese more than a century earlier, and the latter had come to like it as well as understand it. Consequently, the South Vietnamese judge advocates did not see why their system should be changed to suit the Americans. Eblen concluded that any further "Americanization" of the Vietnamese military justice system should be a low priority. Believing instead that "cooperation and good relations" between the Vietnamese and Americans were of greater importance, Eblen ceased working on a new Vietnamese military code. To assist in MAAG advisory efforts, however, Eblen had his office translate the Vietnamese penal code from French into English, forwarding a copy of it to the newly established Foreign Law Branch in the Office of the Judge Advocate General in Washington, D.C., when that office requested a copy.[30]

Lawyering at the Military Assistance Command, Vietnam, and U.S. Army Support Group, Vietnam

The creation of the MACV as a unified command in February 1962, and the establishment one month later of the U.S. Army Support Group, Vietnam, as the Army component under MACV headquarters heralded a much greater commitment of men and materiel to Vietnam, including lawyers. Personnel changes in the legal community reflected this stepped-up commitment.

In August 1962, Lt. Col. Eblen was replaced by Lt. Col. George F. Westerman. An international law expert who would later serve as the chief of the International Affairs Division in the Office of the Judge Advocate General, Westerman provided legal advice to both MAAG and MACV headquarters. Including Maj. Wright and 1st Lt. Graves, who remained at the advisory group, there now were three Army lawyers in Saigon. A year later, in 1963, Westerman, Wright, and Graves were replaced by three other Army lawyers, Lt. Col. Richard L. Jones, Maj. William G. Myers, and Capt. John A. Zalonis. Like their

13

predecessors, all three men were assigned to the advisory group but served both MAAG and MACV headquarters.

With the disestablishment of the MAAG in May 1964, Lt. Col. Robert J. DeMund, who had replaced Lt. Col. Jones in December 1963, became the first MACV staff judge advocate. Lt. Col. George R. Robinson was scheduled to follow DeMund as the top lawyer in Vietnam, but DeMund had, prior to his departure, recommended that the position be upgraded, and the MACV commander, Gen. William C. Westmoreland, agreed. Consequently, Lt. Col. Robinson, who arrived in November 1964, was quickly followed by Col. George S. Prugh. Prugh not only was the first "bird" colonel lawyer at headquarters but also the first MACV staff judge advocate to have graduated from the Army War College. Robinson, however, very much wanted to serve in Vietnam, so he willingly took over as MACV claims judge advocate from Maj. Myers. Rounding out the MACV office were an Air Force judge advocate and a Navy lawyer. Prugh, Robinson, and those two lawyers made up the entire office.

Complementing the lawyer buildup at the advisory group and assistance command was the addition of an Army attorney to the U.S. Army Support Group. Its first judge advocate, Capt. Arthur H. Taylor, arrived in September 1962 and acted as a one-man legal adviser to the brigadier general in command. After Taylors's departure and the unit's redesignation as the U. S. Army Support Command, Vietnam, a lone judge advocate continued to be assigned to it. This ensured that the general officer in command had ready access to a lawyer and legal counsel.

Work at MACV and the support group headquarters was routine, with office hours from 0730 to 1830 or 1930 every night except Sunday, when the offices closed about 1600. Life in Vietnam, although increasingly insecure, still was relatively pleasant. Army lawyers on a twelve-month tour lived in bachelor officers quarters such as the Brink Hotel in Saigon, with life outside of work centering on the officers club and 10-cents-a-glass beer. Some at MACV headquarters, however, continued to serve accompanied two-year tours. Col. Prugh, for example, was accompanied by his family and was "quickly established" in a Chinese villa "with a fine garden and all of the modern conveniences."[31] His daughter enrolled in the American Dependents School and his wife set up housekeeping with the help of a Vietnamese cook and maid. But Prugh was the last judge advocate officially to have his family with him; the Brink bombing on Christmas Eve 1964 and subsequent guerrilla attacks on U.S. forces at Pleiku and Qui Nhon resulted in the return of all dependents to the United States in February 1965.

Expanded Legal Services

From mid-1962 to early 1965, the staff judge advocate's operation at MACV was so small that there was minimal formal organization. Col. Prugh did designate specific areas of responsibility, and his organization was located on the third floor of the Tax Building on Nguyen-Hue Street in Saigon.

Prugh tasked Lt. Col. Robinson with the claims mission. His Navy lawyer, the sole legal assistance officer, also had responsibility for administrative law and international affairs. Prugh's Air Force judge advocate was a one-man military justice and discipline operation. All four attorneys, however, did some legal assistance, and all were called upon to provide command legal advice. Additionally, Col. Prugh served as the legal adviser to the U.S. embassy, U.S. Information Service, and U.S. Agency for International Development, as these organizations did not have their own lawyers in Vietnam.

MACV lawyers advised the command on nonjudicial proceedings under Article 15 of the Uniform Code. A few summary and special courts-martial were convened in Vietnam but, because of the continuing issue of Vietnamese sovereignty, no general courts-martial were conducted. Consequently, when a member of the Army committed a criminal offense requiring disposition by general court, the lawyers at MACV headquarters preferred the charges, conducted the Article 32 investigation, and then forwarded the packet to the U.S. Army, Ryukyu Islands, on Okinawa, the next higher Army headquarters. That general court-martial convening authority referred the case to trial and held the proceedings there. In mid-1962, Capt. Ronald M. Holdaway, later to serve in Vietnam as staff judge advocate of the 1st Cavalry Division, traveled from Hawaii to Okinawa to serve as defense counsel in general courts-martial originating in Vietnam.[32]

The full-time claims judge advocate at MACV headquarters was very busy. The experiences of Maj. William Myers illustrate early claims work in Vietnam. Myers, arriving in December 1963 as the replacement for Capt. Zalonis, had prior service as a World War II naval officer at Iwo Jima and Okinawa. He then transferred to the Army and, after service as an artilleryman with the 1st Cavalry Division in the Korean War, went to law school at Army expense from 1952 to 1955. After a stint as an Army lawyer in France, and then as a legal adviser in

Lebanon during the 1958 U.S. intervention, Myers arrived in Saigon as an experienced military lawyer.

Myers handled all monetary claims filed in Vietnam and payable under the Personnel Claims Act, Military Claims Act, or Foreign Claims Act. The Personnel Claims Act allowed claims by soldiers for damages to or loss of their personal property incident to their service, including combat damage or loss. The Military Claims Act permitted claims by family members of MACV personnel for damages caused by the fault of military personnel or Army civilians acting within the scope of their employment, but the negligence or fault had to be noncombat-related. Finally, the Foreign Claims Act allowed claims by Vietnamese nationals for damages for personal injury, death, or property damage caused by U.S. personnel. The claims, however, had to result from noncombat negligence or other fault; claims for combat-related damage were not payable under the Foreign Claims Act. An example of a claim handled by Maj. Myers involved combat damage to a U.S. adviser's camera. The man had his camera in his rucksack, which was strapped to the side of a South Vietnamese tank. The tank ran over a mine, and a piece of shrapnel went through the camera's lens. The adviser filed a claim for property damage under the Personnel Claims Act. Initially, Lt. Col. DeMund resisted approving the claim, believing that the damage was not incident to service because the adviser had no need for a camera in the field. When the senior U.S. adviser in the area insisted that his advisers carried cameras for intelligence purposes, the claim was approved.[33]

Although claims were filed under the Personnel Claims Act and Military Claims Act, the most serious claims handled by Maj. Myers and claims judge advocates before and after him were those filed by the Vietnamese under the Foreign Claims Act. Most were for property damage or personal injury suffered in traffic accidents involving MACV vehicles. As a one-man foreign claims commission, Myers had authority under that statute to pay any foreign claim up to $1,000. Meritorious claims were settled promptly, as this promoted friendly relations between U.S. forces and the Vietnamese.

From 1962 to 1965 Capts. Taylor, Baldree, and McNamee served at the Army component command headquarters. Capt. Taylor, the first lawyer at the U.S. Army Support Group, arrived in September 1962. After serving as an infantry officer in the United States and Germany, Taylor transferred to the Judge Advocate General's Corps and, after three years' experience as an Army lawyer, found himself as the sole lawyer on Brig. Gen. Joseph W. Stilwell Jr.'s staff. Working conditions were less than ideal. Taylor's office was in a tent and, without air conditioning, paperwork was quickly covered with sweat. Paper clips rusted so quickly in the climate that they could be used only once. The frayed electrical wire strung through Taylor's tent provided a power source, but it also caused the canvas cloth to catch fire. On several occasions, Taylor and his colleagues would organize a fire brigade—emptying their wastepaper baskets, filling them with water from an animal watering trough, and dousing the fire. Security also was a concern. Shortly after arriving, Taylor learned that a Viet Cong attack was imminent. When he went to draw a weapon from the support command armorer, however, Taylor discovered that there were no weapons. He had his brother in the United States send him a .45-caliber semiautomatic pistol in the mail.[34]

Although the support group headquarters was at Tan Son Nhut airport in Saigon, Army elements were based throughout South Vietnam and Thailand. This meant that Taylor frequently journeyed by helicopter and airplane as far north as Da Nang and as far east as Bangkok to provide legal advice to the command and its soldiers. Most of his work concerned military justice and legal assistance. Brig.Gen. Stilwell became a special court-martial convening authority shortly after Taylor's arrival, and Taylor was soon conducting legal reviews of the special courts-martial convened during his stay. Capt. Taylor's biggest job, however, was getting the word out to commanders about the new amendments to Article 15 of the Uniform Code. Congress amended that article in 1962 by increasing a commander's power to punish nonjudicially, thus providing a better alternative to trial by court-martial for minor offenses. Previously, for example, a commander did not have the authority to impose forfeiture of pay on enlisted personnel at an Article 15 proceeding. The 1962 amendments, however, allowed a forfeiture of from seven days' pay to one-half of one month's pay for two months, depending on the grade of the officer imposing the punishment. As a result of these changes, Taylor had an airplane assigned to him for travel throughout Vietnam to apprise Army personnel of the amendments. Using the plane required that Taylor learn the rudiments of flying. A few months earlier, a pilot had been shot while flying a mission and the passenger in the rear seat was required to fly and land the plane. Should a similar emergency occur with Taylor on board, he would be better prepared.[35]

Capt. Taylor returned to the United States in 1963 and was replaced by Capt. Baldree. When the latter left in June 1964, his replacement was Capt. McNamee. A former infantry officer with service in the 82d

Airborne Division, 5th Infantry Division, and 10th Special Forces Group before entering the Judge Advocate General's Corps in 1963, McNamee quickly discovered that his new boss, Brig. Gen. Stilwell, required more than good lawyering from his legal adviser. The son and namesake of Lt. Gen. Joseph W. Stilwell of World War II fame, the younger Stilwell asked his staff officers to serve as door gunners on helicopter missions. With some encouragement, McNamee volunteered.

After Stilwell's departure a few months later, Capt. McNamee discovered that his new boss, Gen. Oden, had a different perspective on a judge advocate's role. Oden not only looked to McNamee for legal advice, but also tasked him with solving nonlegal problems. For example, U.S. Army troops in Vietnam were not receiving hostile-fire pay, although some were being wounded and killed in combat operations. After researching the issue, McNamee advised Gen. Oden that hostile-fire pay could and should be paid, and he drafted a memorandum for the latter that went to MACV headquarters. The result was that hostile-fire pay was approved for soldiers in Vietnam. For this and other excellent staff work, McNamee received the Legion of Merit.[36]

New Issues

When Col. Prugh arrived at MACV headquarters around Thanksgiving 1964, he brought with him superb credentials. With World War II service as an artillery officer in New Guinea and the Philippines, Prugh appreciated the difficulties facing the MACV command and staff. Having been a judge advocate since 1949, with three previous tours in the Pentagon and overseas lawyering in Germany and Korea, Prugh was also adept at handling legal policy questions at a high level. Perhaps this explains why he immediately saw three major issues in Vietnam requiring lawyer involvement. The first involved prisoners of war, the second concerned war crimes, and the third dealt with resources control.

By the end of 1964, more than 24,000 American soldiers were in Vietnam. As some of these men were participating in combat operations, it was inevitable that a few were captured by the enemy. What was happening to these Americans? Although some survived, Col. Prugh learned that it was more likely for the Viet Cong to kill them rather than take them prisoner. One captured American adviser, for example, had been beheaded and his head displayed on a pole. Another had had his hands tied behind his back before being shot in the head. Having obtained permission from Gen. Westmoreland to question soldiers departing Vietnam at the end of their advisory tours, Prugh learned that both sides—Viet Cong and South Vietnamese—often killed enemy wounded and those captured. The fratricidal nature of the war explained these killings, at least in part. Some guerrillas were executed by the South Vietnamese, however, because the latter viewed them as "Communist rebel combat captives" deserving summary treatment as illegitimate insurgents acting against a legitimate government. In short, the government initially refused to treat Viet Cong captives as prisoners of war. Rather, as prisoner of war status afforded by the *Geneva Convention Relative to the Treatment of Prisoners of War* applies only in armed conflict between states, and as the fighting in Vietnam was regarded by the South Vietnam government as a civil insurrection, the Saigon government insisted that the Geneva Convention was inapplicable and that captured enemy personnel were not entitled to prisoner of war status. Thus, those guerrillas who did survive capture in the field were not sent to prisoner of war camps. Instead, they were imprisoned "in provincial and national jails along with political prisoners and common criminals."[37] In sum, the government viewed the enemy as criminals and treated them accordingly. The Viet Cong, however, were usually even harsher in their treatment of captives, executing South Vietnamese soldiers falling into their hands as a matter of routine. Initially, captured U.S. advisers were spared, but when the government of South Vietnam publicly executed some enemy agents, the Viet Cong killed captured U.S. advisers in retribution.[38]

Col. Prugh and his legal staff quickly realized that American advisers captured in South Vietnam and pilots shot down and taken prisoner in North Vietnam would not survive captivity unless these men received prisoner of war status. Believing that the Viet Cong and North Vietnamese might reciprocate with better treatment of U.S. captives if South Vietnam were to reverse its position on the status of Viet Cong prisoners, Prugh and his staff worked to convince Col. Nguyen Monh Bich, the Director of Military Justice, that it was in South Vietnam's best interest to construct prison camps for enemy captives and to ensure their humane treatment during imprisonment. The more enemy prisoners of war there were in custody, the more likely that an exchange of South Vietnamese and American prisoners of war could be worked out. Additionally, a unilateral decision by the Saigon government to acknowledge the applicability of the *Geneva*

Convention Relative to the Treatment of Prisoners of War "would also ameliorate domestic and international criticism of the war."[39]

In December 1964, Col. Prugh and Col. Bich visited Vietnamese confinement facilities throughout South Vietnam. By American standards, conditions were very poor—overcrowding, insufficient food, and a shortage of qualified security personnel prevailed. In Da Nang, for example, Prugh saw that one jail, built by the French to house 250 individuals, in fact had some 750 people incarcerated in it. Not only were far too many people locked up in the facility, but also combat captives were mingled with prostitutes, thieves, and other criminals, along with juveniles, popularly known as "slicky boys" because of their streetwise ways.[40]

In the end, persuading the South Vietnamese to reverse course was agonizingly slow. Yet by mid-1966, the South Vietnamese had set up facilities suitable for confinement of prisoners of war, and the number of such prisoners held by South Vietnam went from zero to nearly 36,000 by the end of 1971. Prugh and the judge advocates who followed him deserve much of the credit for reversing South Vietnam's "no POW" policy and the resulting better treatment for enemy prisoners of war. Unfortunately, the Viet Cong and North Vietnamese did not acknowledge the applicability of the Geneva Convention, and their treatment of American and South Vietnamese captives continued to be brutal. But, as more U.S. troops were surviving capture and the humane treatment afforded Viet Cong and North Vietnamese Army prisoners exerted constant pressure on the enemy to reciprocate, Col. Prugh's initiative was of real benefit.[41]

The second issue of critical importance to Prugh was the formulation of a policy on war crimes investigations. When Prugh arrived in 1964, the American command had no official policy on how violations of the Law of War should be investigated or on who should conduct such investigations. Believing that the command not only needed "uniform procedures for the collection . . . of evidence relative to war crimes incidents" but that it also must "designate the agencies responsible for the conduct of [such] investigations," Prugh authored MACV Directive 20–4, *Inspections and Investigations of War Crimes*.[42] In preparing the directive in early 1965, he looked to an old memorandum on war crimes reporting authored by Col. (later Maj. Gen.) George W. Hickman during the Korean War, when Hickman was staff judge advocate of the United Nations Command. Using the Hickman memorandum as his point of departure, Col. Prugh produced a document defining different types of war crimes and prohibited acts and requiring their reporting to the MACV staff judge. Prugh's original MACV Directive 20–4 governed only investigations of war crimes committed against U.S. forces. Subsequently, however, MACV lawyers revised the directive so that it encompassed war crimes committed both by and against U.S. military and civilian personnel in Vietnam. By mid-1965, MACV judge advocates advised on, assisted in, and later reviewed all war crimes investigations in Vietnam. This was a significant responsibility and remained a major mission for MACV lawyers until the end of the war in Vietnam.[43]

The third problem identified by Col. Prugh as needing lawyer involvement concerned resources control in South Vietnam. Believing that the defeat of the enemy would not occur without a "plan of national pacification in the form of the blockade of all enemy sources of supply," the Saigon government issued nearly 100 legal decrees controlling the distribution of resources.[44] Materiel critical to the enemy effort—food, medicine, transport, and other items—was strictly controlled by monitoring its use and by storing excess supply in government-controlled buildings. As the MACV mission was to aid the government in its fight against the insurrection, MACV advisers had to understand all of Saigon's efforts undertaken to win the war. Given that the principal method for controlling the supply and distribution of resources was by enacting a series of laws and prosecuting violators in the South Vietnamese military courts, MACV judge advocates naturally were the focal point for intelligent advice on resources control. Effective advising, however, meant collecting, translating, indexing, interpreting, mimeographing, and distributing all relevant government decrees and directives. It also meant learning how resources control really worked so that practical guidance could be distributed to U.S. advisers in the field.

MACV lawyers soon recognized that they had to be familiar with all Vietnamese laws having a bearing on the conduct of the war. This required understanding the entire Vietnamese legal system and keeping abreast of changes affecting more than just resources control. For American-trained lawyers, this was no easy task. For example, Vietnamese law made no distinction between criminal and civil matters, important in Anglo-American jurisprudence. The Vietnamese civilian court system existed side-by-side with its military court system, but the latter exercised extremely broad jurisdiction, as all offenses against state security were prosecuted in military courts. Consequently, as any breach of a resources control law was a crime against state security, this meant that both civilian and military offenders were prosecuted in military courts. Again, for U.S.-schooled judge advocates, this was an important point, given that American courts-martial generally lack jurisdiction over civilian offenders. MACV judge advocates quickly learned that advising on resources control required synthesizing various Vietnamese laws and decrees and then disseminating that information to nonlawyer U.S. advisers. While some compilation of Vietnamese law had been done by early judge advocate advisers, major efforts in gathering and distributing information on Vietnamese law occurred only after 1965, when additional personnel assigned to Col. Prugh's office in Saigon meant more manpower was available for this task.[45]

Army Lawyers on the Eve of the Intervention

The arrival of the 173d Airborne Brigade (Separate) in May 1965 marked the end of relatively small U.S. Army involvement in Vietnam and the beginning of direct intervention. The role of Army lawyers in Vietnam from 1959 to 1965 reflected the limited mission in the early period. Military justice, claims, legal assistance, administrative law—traditional military lawyering—were done by a single judge advocate or a small legal operation. Judge advocates in Vietnam also served as advisers to the South Vietnamese. With no previous experience or model to follow, Army lawyers created an advisory program that directly supported the war effort. Advising began with teaching American jurisprudence and learning about Vietnamese law. Later, it included spearheading efforts to gain prisoner of war status for enemy soldiers. In November 1965 when South Vietnam accepted the applicability of the Geneva Convention to the fighting in Vietnam, it was not only a major victory for the rule of law in war, but also an enhanced opportunity for survival for U.S. personnel in enemy hands.

The eve of the intervention, then, found Army lawyers in Vietnam doing both their traditional legal service and important advisory work. The coming years would transform the role and mission of the U.S. Army in Vietnam. More soldiers and more units would mean more lawyers, but the intervention resulted in more than rapid growth in the size of the Judge Advocate General's Corps. It also brought major changes in judge advocate operations in combat, particularly in the area of military justice. At the same time, a number of judge advocates continued taking individual initiatives to enhance mission success in nontraditional ways. For some, this would mean taking personal risks as Col. Durbin did in leaving the safety of his home to observe a coup d'etat by disaffected South Vietnamese paratroops. For others, it would mean using legal talents as Col. Prugh did in persuading the South Vietnamese military that the Geneva Convention on Prisoners of War applied to ongoing hostilities, in formulating a policy on war crimes investigations in Vietnam, and in creating the unique advisory program. These individual initiatives showed that a judge advocate could enhance mission success in nontraditional ways and the increasing number of Army lawyers in Southeast Asia showed a corresponding increase in the number of such individual initiatives.

Notes

1. Interv, author with Col Paul J. Durbin, 1 Jul 96, Historians files, Office of the Judge Advocate General (OTJAG), Department of the Army, Washington, D.C.

2. Memorandum no. 10, Missions and Functions of MAAG Advisers, MAAG Hq, 27 Jan 61, box 25, Records of the MAAG Adjutant General Division, Record Group (RG) 334, National Archives and Records Administration (NARA), College Park, Md.

3. Vincent H. Demma, "The U.S. Army in Vietnam," in Maurice Matloff, ed., *American Military History* (Washington, D.C.: Government Printing Office, 1973), 623; Ronald H. Spector, *Advice and Support: The Early Years, 1941–1960, U.S. Army in Vietnam* (Washington, D.C.: Government Printing Office, 1983), 291.

4. Demma, "U.S. Army in Vietnam," 631.

5. MAAG Vietnam Judge Advocate Responsibilities, Appendix I to Annex L (Legal), MAAG Vietnam OPLAN 61–61, 10 Feb 61, box 25, Records of the MAAG Adjutant General Division, RG 334, NARA.

6. Interv, author with Durbin, 1 Jul 96. For an in-depth discussion of the Vietnamese legal system and its French structure, see George S. Prugh, *Law at War: Vietnam 1964–1973*, Vietnam Studies (Washington, D.C.: Government Printing Office, 1974), 15–39.

7. Interv, author with Durbin, 1 Jul 96.

8. Ibid.

9. Interv, author with Col George C. Eblen, 23 Aug 96, Historians files, OTJAG.

10. DF, MAAG Hq, 25 Aug 60, sub: Investigation-M/SGT Price, box 23, Records of the MAAG Adjutant General Division, RG 334, NARA.

11. Interv, author with Durbin, 1 Jul 96.

12. Ibid.

13. Spector, *The Early Years*, 370.

14. Interv, author with Durbin, 1 Jul 96.

15. MAAG Vietnam OPLAN 61–61, Annex L (Legal).

16. Ibid.

17. Ibid.

18. Ibid.

19. Ibid.

20. Interv, author with Eblen, 9 Sep 96, Historians files, OTJAG.

21. Ibid.

22. Memo for Record, MACV Hq, 17 Jul 62, sub: Status of Forces in Thailand, Historians files, OTJAG; interv, author with Eblen, 9 Sep 96.

23. Interv, author with Eblen, 23 Aug 96; Prugh, *Law at War*, 98.

24. Interv, author with Durbin, 1 Jul 96.

25. Prugh, *Law at War*, 46.

26. Ibid., 47.

27. Staff Study, MACV Hq, "Purpose: To examine the role of the Civil Law in counterinsurgency in Vietnam and to make pertinent recommendations," 31 May 65, p. 3, Historians files, OTJAG.

28. Interv, author with Durbin, 1 Jul 96. See also Prugh, *Law at War*, 41.

29. Interv, author with Col Paul J. Durbin, 16 Aug 96, Historians files, OTJAG.

30. Interv, author with Eblen, 9 Sep 96.

31. Ltr, Prugh to Col Thomas H. Swan, 26 Apr 65, Historians files, OTJAG.

32. Interv, author with Ronald M. Holdaway, 24 Jul 96, Historians files, OTJAG.

33. Interv, author with Lt Col William G. Myers, 15 Jul 96, Historians files, OTJAG.

34. Interv, author with Arthur H. Taylor, 2 Aug 96, Historians files, OTJAG.

35. Ibid.; interv, author with Arthur H. Taylor, 21 Nov 96, Historians files, OTJAG.

36. Interv, author with Alfred A. McNamee, 31 Jul 96, Historians files, OTJAG.

37. Jeffrey J. Clarke, *Advice and Support: The Final Years, 1965–1973, U.S. Army in Vietnam* (Washington, D.C.: Government Printing Office, 1987), 119.

38. Prugh, *Law at War*, 63.

39. Clarke, *The Final Years*, 120.

40. Prugh, *Law at War*, 63; interv, author with Prugh, 31 Jul 96, Historians files, OTJAG.

41. Prugh, *Law at War*, 61–67; Clarke, *The Final Years*, 170.

42. MACV Directive 20–4, *Inspections and Investigations of War Crimes*, 20 Apr 65, Historians files, OTJAG.

43. Prugh, *Law at War*, 72–73.

44. Memo, MACV Hq, 21 Jan 65, sub: Resources Control, Arrest, Search, and Seizure Laws in the Republic of Vietnam, Incl 2, 1, Historians files, OTJAG.

45. Prugh, *Law at War*, 42; interv, author with Prugh, 31 Jul 96.

Chapter 2

Vietnam: Military Law During the Offensive 1965-1969

"Every Staff Judge Advocate should ask two questions: What should I do to keep my command obedient to the law? What can the law do to further the mission of the command? In Vietnam, the second question kept us the busiest."[1]

—Maj. Gen. George Prugh, Staff Judge Advocate, Military Assistance Command, Vietnam (1964-1966)

Background

Once the decision was taken to intervene with ground troops, in the spring of 1965, policy and battlefield patterns were set that would see the United States through the next four years of war. When the year began, there was still some hope, although rapidly diminishing, that an expansion in advice and support operations short of ground forces would enable Vietnam to weather the most recent upsurge from the Viet Cong. That advice and support option evaporated quickly when a series of South Vietnamese battle defeats raised the specter of collapse. From that point on, unwilling to accept the consequences of a Communist victory that seemed ever more likely, the Johnson administration started pouring men and materiel into Vietnam; the war for that nation, hitherto limited, turned into high drama for the United States.

In entering upon this course of escalation and perseverance, no source of military pressure was overlooked. The bombing of North Vietnam, begun in February, was one prong of an evolving American war strategy. Support for Saigon's pacification effort in the countryside was a second prong and increased in importance as time went on. Nevertheless, the main focus of the American intervention was ground combat against the enemy's main forces wherever they could be found. In furthering that mission while managing an ever-expanding ground war by maneuver elements of the U.S. Army and Marine Corps, Gen. Westmoreland and MACV headquarters held center stage.[2]

Westmoreland's instruments for exercising operational control over U.S. ground forces started with three corps-size commands in the field-I Field Force and II Field Force for U.S. Army units, and III

Marine Amphibious Force for the Marines. The field forces were the senior Army tactical commands in country, and they reported directly to Westmoreland in Saigon. However, while exercising operational control over U.S. units (and any Australian, Korean, or other Free World forces subordinate to them), the two field forces were "to maintain close liaison with MACV's senior advisers with Vietnamese troops" and coordinate with Vietnamese Army corps commanders in their areas of operation.[3] In theory, Westmoreland tasked a field force with a particular mission, and it in turn selected one or more subordinate divisions or a separate brigade to conduct the operation. In practice, Westmoreland often went directly to his divisions, because the units and personalities involved in an operation determined who would do the actual planning or exercise control of it.

All Army units arriving in Vietnam were assigned to USARV, the service component, which exercised command less operational control of combat forces and was headed by the senior Army three-star in Vietnam. Established in July 1965, the USARV command grew rapidly-a burgeoning establishment of logistical, engineer, signal, medical, military police, and aviation units driving the escalation in manpower. And the numbers tell the story: of the Army's eighteen divisions, seven were in Vietnam by the end of 1967.[4] These divisions were the 1st Cavalry Division (Airmobile); the 1st, 4th, 9th, 23d, and 25th Infantry Divisions; and the 101st Airborne Division. The 23d Infantry (American) Division was formed in Vietnam as an amalgamation of the 11th, 196th, and 198th Light Infantry Brigades. At the peak of the buildup in early 1969, there were 543,000 U.S. troops from all the services in Vietnam, including recently deployed units such as the 3d Brigade, 82d Airborne Division, and the 1st Brigade, 5th Infantry Division (Mechanized). Joining these soldiers were some 1,100 U.S. civilian employees of the Department of Defense and about 9,000 U.S. civilian employees of U.S. contractors.[5]

Military operations in Vietnam ranged from large-scale battles against main force Viet Cong and North Vietnamese units to platoon- and company-size operations. Regardless of the size of the operation, all fell into one of three categories: search and destroy operations against large enemy units, clearing operations to force guerrilla units out of an area, and securing operations to destroy the remaining enemy.[6] Operation ATTLEBORO, for example, started as a small search and destroy operation in the II Field Force area north of Saigon, but grew into a massive offensive involving twenty-one battalions from the 196th Infantry Brigade; the 173d Airborne Brigade; the 1st, 4th, and

25th Infantry Divisions; and the 11th Armored Cavalry Regiment. Control of ATTLEBORO passed from the 196th Brigade to the 1st Division and finally to II Field Force as some 22,000 troops became involved.

ATTLEBORO and operations like it, however, were the clear exception. The typical U.S. Army division or separate brigade had a designated area of operations, usually covering several Vietnamese provinces within one of the four Vietnamese corps areas, in which subordinate elements sought out the enemy's forces. The 1st Cavalry Division in 1969 illustrates how a typical division operated. Its main headquarters, location of the commanding general and his principal staff, was north of Saigon at Phuoc Vinh, protected by a battalion-size "palace guard." The division rear headquarters was at Bien Hoa, location of most of its logistical and administrative support. The 1st Cavalry's three brigades with their respective headquarters were

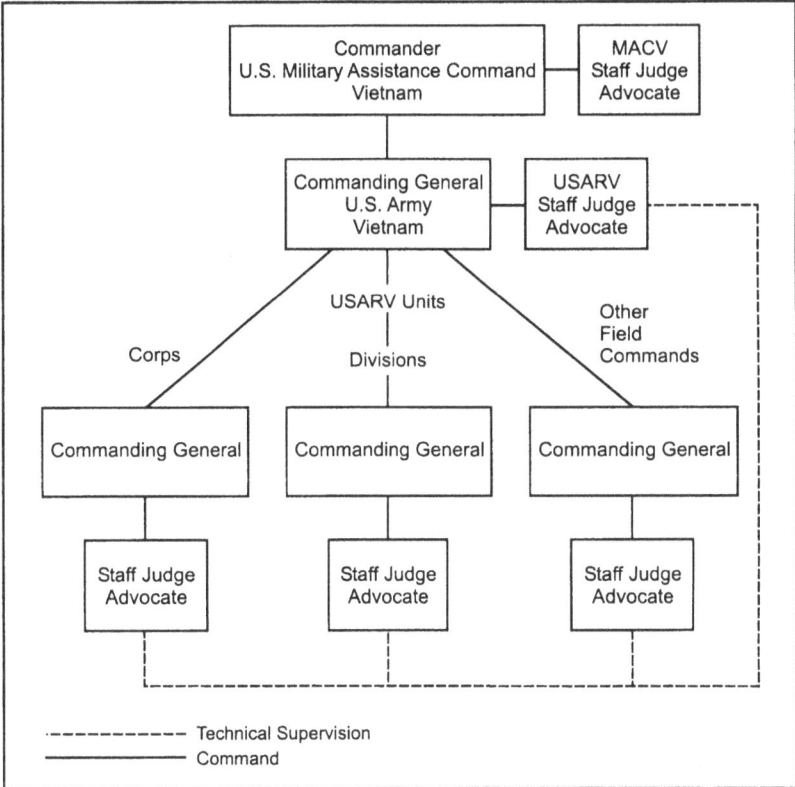

Figure 1. Legal organization of U.S. Army units in Vietnam (1965-1972)

dispersed at three different base camps located 50 to 100 miles from each other. Battalions in these brigades were located at still other bases, usually settled in with artillery, and the battalions themselves were often dispersed into two or three smaller bases. In sum, the 1st Cavalry Division was spread out among a dozen or more base camps and firebases. While the division and brigade bases were fairly permanent in location, the firebases were not, opening or closing depending on the division's mission. Helicopters linked the firebases, ferrying troops, supplies, and equipment to and from them. Platoon- and company-size elements left their firebases-either on foot or by air-to conduct operations. Most combat operations in Vietnam were never larger than company size. Many were run at night.[7]

Measured by traditional military standards, the offensive against the Viet Cong and North Vietnamese Army was successful, with high enemy body counts (as many as ten enemy dead for every U.S. casualty); large seizures of weapons, ammunition, food, and other vital materiel; and repeated destruction of enemy base camps, bunkers, and tunnel networks. That said, no matter how deeply U.S. forces ranged into hostile territory, the enemy reorganized and reappeared on the battlefield.

From 1965 to 1969, the number of Army lawyers in Vietnam mirrored the ground combat buildup. There were four Army lawyers in Vietnam-three at MACV and one at the support command-in early 1965. By 1969, there were more than 135 U.S. Army attorneys there.[8] From 1965 to 1969, lawyers served at the headquarters of MACV; USARV; I and II Field Forces; and every division and separate brigade, as well as a number of large support organizations such as transportation and engineer commands. Figure 1 illustrates the legal organization of U.S. Army units in Vietnam between 1965 and 1972.

Lawyering at MACV

In early 1965, the MACV staff judge advocate's office provided the full range of legal services-from claims, legal assistance, and military justice to international law, Law of War, and administrative law. It also advised the Vietnamese Director of Military Justice and his staff. The arrival of the first U.S. combat units in the spring and summer of that year transformed the command's legal operations and resulted in the disappearance of certain of these traditional lawyering tasks. By late 1966, for example, the MACV staff judge advocate had transferred responsibility for claims adjudication to USARV. Additionally, the command no longer convened courts-martial; prosecuting and defending cases were left to USARV judge advocates and military lawyers assigned to its subordinate units. Consequently, by 1967, the MACV legal office had a slimmed-down organizational structure: a Civil Law and Military Affairs Division, a Criminal and International Law Division, and an Advisory Division. In the Civil Law and Military Affairs Division, MACV judge advocates advised on currency control, black marketeering, withdrawal of privileges from civilian contractor employees, denial of access to military installations and facilities to U.S. civilians, and determinations of unacceptability for employment under U.S. government contracts. The same division also advised on real estate matters such as compensating owners for land appropriated for use as a military base or facility and negotiating commercial leases of property (there were more than 1,300 such leases in Saigon alone by 1970). The Civil Law and Military Affairs Division also advised the Central Purchasing Agency, Vietnam, on importing, distributing, and selling all post exchange items in Vietnam.

MACV's Criminal and International Law Division furnished "advice and guidance" to subordinate commands in the disposition of disciplinary and criminal matters. In the area of international law, the division maintained files of war crimes investigations and gave opinions on the Geneva Conventions and Laws of War.[9] The Advisory Division coordinated with the Vietnamese Directorate of Military Justice and participated in legal society and educational programs in Saigon. It also monitored the activities of its judge advocate field advisers. These lawyers worked in all four Vietnamese corps areas on a wide variety of legal issues ranging from desertion control, resources control, and security operations to obtaining transportation for Vietnamese judge advocates, providing storage for records of trials, and obtaining materiel for local prisons.[10]

Rounding out the MACV legal operation were one or more Vietnamese attorney-advisers and interpreter-translators. An Administrative Division provided clerical and other administrative support for the office. MACV's multiservice composition meant that one or more Air Force and Navy judge advocates were always part of the MACV legal staff, acting as liaisons with their respective services in addition to the legal tasks given them by the MACV staff judge advocate. As it happened, the latter remained an Army colonel because Army personnel were always the largest MACV component.

The number of Army attorneys at MACV headquarters ranged from a low of three in 1965 to a high of nine in 1967. In early 1967, eight

Army attorneys worked for Staff Judge Advocate Col. Edward W. Haughney. They were Lt. Cols. Robert E. Bjelland, Guy A. Hamlin, and Robert M. Thorniley; Capts. David T. Gray, Philip L. Robins, Robert E. Shoun, and Pedar C. Wold; and 1st Lt. Russell C. Shaw. Joining their Army counterparts at the headquarters were three Navy lawyers and five Air Force lawyers, one of whom was a colonel and served as Haughney's deputy staff judge advocate. Supporting these American attorneys were seven Vietnamese lawyers and some fifty Vietnamese clerks and translators, making a total of about seventy-five people at the MACV staff judge advocate's office. As during Col. Prugh's tenure as MACV staff judge advocate, Col. Haughney and his legal staff worked in the Tax Building in downtown Saigon and lived across the street in the Rex Hotel.[11] Figure 2 shows the organization of the MACV Office of the Staff Judge Advocate in 1967. After that date the number of Army lawyers at MACV headquarters declined.

Legal Policy Issues

By 1967, the MACV staff judge advocate's office was formulating legal policy in three major areas: prisoners of war and war crimes, discipline and criminal law, and claims. Agreed upon policies were promulgated in MACV directives, and over the next few years MACV lawyers wrote and periodically updated more than twenty regulations.

On the subject of prisoners of war and war crimes, MACV continued to develop legal policy based on the Geneva Prisoner of War Convention and U.S. policy. By August 1965, the South Vietnamese accepted the American view that the hostilities constituted an armed international conflict, that North Vietnam was a belligerent, and that the Viet Cong were agents of the government of North Vietnam. Shortly thereafter, the commander of MACV directed that all suspected guerrillas captured by U.S. combat units be treated initially as

Col. Edward W. Haughney, MACV staff judge advocate, 1966-67. Having participated in five campaigns while an artillery captain in France and Germany in World War II, Haughney had a wealth of real world experience. During his 12 month tour in Vietnam, Haughney and his staff used the law to support MACV by promulgating the first procedural framework for classifying prisoners of war.

prisoners of war and that those units be responsible for prisoners from the time of capture until release to Vietnamese authorities. Although MACV could have kept enemy captured by American units in U.S. custody, the decision was made that they would be detained only long enough to interrogate them for tactical intelligence. Thereafter, all prisoners were sent to a combined U.S.-Vietnamese center for classification and further processing by the South Vietnamese. Prisoners of war were sent to prisoner of war camps; innocent civilians were released and returned to the place of capture; civilian defendants were delivered to Vietnamese civil authorities; and guerrillas seeking amnesty under the "Chieu Hoi" or "Open Arms" program were sent to the Chieu Hoi center. Although the Vietnamese authorities took custody of all prisoners of war, Article 12 of the Geneva Prisoner of War Convention still required the United States to ensure that Vietnamese treatment of captives complied with the convention. Consequently, by the end of 1968, MACV lawyers had helped implement a prisoner of war program that established Vietnamese prisoner of war camps and created a repatriation program for prisoners of war.

Although the MACV provost marshal was primarily responsible for advising the Vietnamese on prisoner of war camp issues, MACV judge advocates took the lead on several prisoner of war issues. Most noteworthy was work done during Col. Haughney's tenure as MACV staff judge advocate from July 1966 to July 1967. Haughney and his legal staff promulgated the first procedural framework for classifying combat captives using so-called Article 5 tribunals. Under that article of the Geneva Prisoners of War Convention, a "competent tribunal" of not less than three officers had to be used to determine if a person was entitled to prisoner of war status. MACV Directive 20-5, *Prisoners of War-Determination of Eligibility*, first issued in September 1966 and updated in March 1968, both established and provided authority for a procedural framework for Article 5 tribunals. The directive explained that "the responsibility for determining the status of persons captured by U.S. forces rests with the United States" and that no combat captive or detainee could be transferred to the Vietnamese until "his status as a prisoner of war or non-prisoner of war" was determined. Consequently, a tribunal including at least one lawyer familiar with the Geneva Prisoner of War Convention would hold a formal hearing to decide each doubtful case. No Article 5 tribunal was required for persons who "obviously" were prisoners of war, such as North Vietnamese Army or Viet Cong regulars captured while fighting on the battlefield. An

Article 5 tribunal was needed only for a detained person whose legal status was in doubt. This was often the case in Vietnam because rarely did the Viet Cong wear a recognizable uniform, and only occasionally did the guerrillas carry their arms openly. Additionally, some combat captives were compelled to act for the Viet Cong out of fear of harm to themselves or their families. Despite these complications, the tribunal could still find that such a person was a prisoner of war. Or, it could decide that the person was a "civil defendant" triable in the Vietnamese courts or an innocent civilian who should be released. Detailed guidance on conducting an Article 5 tribunal was contained in Annex A of the directive, including rights of the detainee and counsel, voting procedures, powers of the tribunal, and posthearing procedures. The MACV staff judge advocate reviewed all tribunal decisions "to insure there were no irregularities in the proceedings."[12] In addition to pioneering work done in establishing Article 5 tribunals, MACV lawyers spearheaded efforts establishing a records system identifying and listing all prisoners of war. They also advised their Vietnamese counterparts on the rights of captives to receive mail, medical attention, and Red Cross visits.[13]

In the area of war crimes investigations, the lawyers at MACV continued the work started by their predecessors, setting out detailed written guidance on investigating and reporting war crimes. Significantly, the command decided as a matter of policy that the MACV staff judge advocate-as opposed to the provost marshal or any subordinate headquarters legal officer-would oversee all war crimes matters. Thus, by mid-1968, an updated MACV Directive 20-4, *Inspections and Investigations, War Crimes*, required the reporting of all war crimes committed by or against U.S. forces. All investigations were to be coordinated with MACV lawyers, with technical assistance furnished by qualified criminal investigators. To ensure that MACV members understood what constituted a war crime, the directive listed eighteen examples, including willfully killing, torturing, taking hostages, maltreating dead bodies, pillaging or purposeless destruction, compelling prisoners of war or civilians to perform prohibited labor, and killing without trial persons who had committed hostile acts. Finally, the directive placed special requirements on MACV members. First, any service member having knowledge of an incident thought to be a war crime was required "to make such incident known to his commanding officer as soon as practicable." Additionally, those involved in "investigative, intelligence, police, photographic, grave registration, or medical functions," as well as those in contact with the enemy, were required to "make every effort to detect the commission of war crimes." Finally, MACV Directive 20-4 was punitive, in that disobeying it was a violation of the Uniform Code of Military Justice. This underscored the command's interest in the Law of War, but was particularly significant because American law generally did not make criminal a citizen's failure to report criminal activity to law enforcement authorities. This decision to penalize the failure to report a war crime applied to all levels of command. One of the charges preferred against Maj. Gen. Samuel W. Koster in 1970 was that he had failed to report a high number of civilians killed at My Lai by soldiers under his command. Although this charge and others were later dismissed, Koster's failure to obey MACV Directive 20-4 while commanding the Americal Division was part of the legal basis for the adverse administrative action against him.[14]

By the time American troop strength peaked in 1969, MACV Directive 20-4 and other MACV directives contained a sufficient body of law to define, prohibit, and provide for investigation of war crimes. During this time, the most grievous breaches of the Geneva Conventions were those committed by the enemy, and there were several incidents where U.S. troops were murdered and their bodies mutilated by the Viet Cong or North Vietnamese. The enemy policy of kidnapping civilians and assassinating public officials resulted in particularly vicious crimes. At the same time, American soldiers also committed war crimes, and from 1965 to 1973 there were 241 cases (besides My Lai) alleging war crimes committed by Americans. After investigation, 160 of these were found to be unsubstantiated. Thirty-six war crimes incidents, however, resulted in trials by courts-martial on charges ranging from premeditated murder, rape, and assault with intent to commit murder or rape to involuntary manslaughter, negligent homicide, and the mutilation of enemy dead. Sixteen trials involving thirty men resulted in findings of not guilty or dismissal after arraignment. Twenty cases involving thirty-one soldiers resulted in conviction. Punishments varied. While military law required that a court convicting a soldier of premeditated murder must also impose a punishment of confinement for life, sentences imposed for other offenses depended on the facts and circumstances of each case. Thus, a rape conviction invariably carried with it a dishonorable or bad conduct discharge and one to ten years' confinement. A conviction for involuntary manslaughter or negligent homicide usually meant a punitive discharge and some period of confinement at hard labor. In at least one court case, however, a soldier convicted of involuntary manslaughter received only an admonishment. And a sergeant found guilty of cutting off the heads of two dead enemy soldiers and posing for photographs with the bodies was sentenced only to a reduction in grade.[15]

In the area of discipline and criminal law, MACV developed criminal law policy in two major areas. First, it implemented a coherent program for dealing with misconduct committed by MACV members as well as U.S. civilians connected with the war effort. Second, MACV judge advocates worked with other U.S. government agencies in Vietnam in suppressing black-marketeering and similar irregular practices.

In regard to command policy on controlling misconduct by MACV members, basic guidance was contained in MACV Directive 27-6, Legal Services and Legal Obligations in Vietnam, first issued on 16 June 1965 and later updated on 14 September 1968, and in MACV Directive 27-4, *Legal Services: Foreign Jurisdiction Procedures and Information*, 2 November 1967. These directives set out the command's policy on compliance with Vietnamese law, with the goal of minimizing conflict between MACV troops and Vietnamese law enforcement authorities.[16] Thus, while acknowledging that all U.S. troops had immunity from Vietnamese civil and criminal law, Directive 27-6 required compliance with Vietnamese law, "including traffic laws and law pertaining to curfews, off-limits areas, and currency." U.S. personnel, whether military or civilian, "were to comply and cooperate" with Vietnamese law enforcement authorities and "under no circumstances . . . were to resist by force."[17]

A particularly thorny legal policy issue was criminal activity by U.S. civilians. Such misconduct fell into three categories: disorderly conduct, abuse of military privileges, and black-market activities and currency manipulation. In April 1966, at the request of the U.S. ambassador, the MACV staff judge advocate prepared a staff study on the ambassador's authority over U.S. civilians in Vietnam. That study concluded that the ambassador could issue police regulations for all U.S. citizens in Vietnam if the regulations did not conflict with U.S. or Vietnamese laws.[18] The study also concluded that armed forces police could be used to enforce those regulations. Civilians who violated Vietnamese or American laws were punished using administrative measures, such as withdrawal of military privileges and loss of employment. The increase in serious crimes committed by U.S. civilians, however, soon made criminal prosecutions appropriate. But who would prosecute? Although some American laws have extraterritorial application, there were really only two practical possibilities: the U.S. military or Vietnamese civilian authorities. While American military authorities could exercise control over uniformed personnel using the Uniform Code of Military Justice or MACV directives, their authority over civilians in Vietnam was tenuous at best. Although Article 2 of the Uniform Code did permit the courts-martial of civilians "accompanying an armed force in the field," that provision applied only "in time of war," and it was not clear if the fighting in Vietnam qualified as such. Additionally, even if U.S. military operations did so qualify, criminal jurisdiction over civilians extended only to those civilians accompanying U.S. forces "in the field." Consequently, while civilian employees of government contractors engaged in military projects, war correspondents with troops on combat missions, and merchant sailors unloading cargo in U.S. Army ports might be subject to military criminal jurisdiction, the more than 6,000 U.S. civilian employees of private contractors, independent businessmen, and tourists in Vietnam were not subject to the Uniform Code under any circumstances. In formulating a policy on civilian criminal conduct, however, MACV lawyers found the Vietnamese either unable or unwilling to prosecute these Americans. First, as South Vietnam had been in continual combat since 1956, there was considerable disorganization in the administration of justice. This made prosecution difficult, particularly where legal proof was not easily obtained, as in black-marketing and currency manipulation cases. Second, Vietnamese judicial officials relied on fines and forfeitures for a substantial portion of their income. If a case offered little or no opportunity for financial return, the South Vietnamese had little interest in prosecuting. This was particularly true with many crimes committed by U.S. civilians; if the injured party was an American or the U.S. government, any financial recovery would go to them and not to the Republic of Vietnam.

As a result, the MACV staff judge advocate devised a two-pronged approach to civilian misconduct. First, administrative sanctions were meted out to punish and deter civilian wrongdoing. Withdrawing privileges of a civilian to use the post exchange and commissary, or denying him or her entry onto military bases along with notification to the employer that this official action was being taken, meant that the civilian offender would be returned to the United States immediately by his or her employer.[19] For example, the 34th General Support Group had 1,200 contract aircraft maintenance personnel in Saigon in 1967. Disciplinary problems resulted in termination of the employee by the contractor. As a condition of employment, employees pledged to return to the United States "by the most expeditious means possible"; therefore, troublesome employees were at least out of the country. Other than the loss of employment, however, return to the United States did nothing to punish the offender. Moreover, if an employee refused to leave Vietnam, American authorities could do little, other than ask the Vietnamese to deport him.[20] Consequently, this preference for administrative sanctions to resolve civilian misconduct was complemented with a second MACV policy allowing, when absolutely necessary, military prosecutions of civilians accompanying U.S. forces. With the approval of Ambassador Henry Cabot Lodge, a few such civilian cases were prosecuted by U.S. Army, Vietnam, and 1st Logistical Command, but this practice ceased in 1970 after the U.S. Court of Military Appeals held that there was no military criminal jurisdiction over civilians in Vietnam.[21]

To curb American criminal activity in Vietnam, MACV judge advocates worked with the Irregular Practices Committee. Formed in August 1967 and consisting of three U.S. embassy representatives and the MACV staff judge advocate, the committee had no operational resources. Rather, it coordinated the work of those elements of the U.S. Mission—like the Military Assistance Command—that had resources to suppress black-marketing, currency manipulation, and other illegal activities adversely affecting the Vietnamese economy. Initially, the committee focused on Vietnamese complaints about black-marketing by U.S. forces. With the arrival of American combat units, the Army and Air Force exchange system expanded dramatically. At the end of 1966, for example, there were 146 U.S. retail exchange outlets in Vietnam with a net income of $160 million. A year later, there were 304 retail outlets. These exchange outlets sold soap, toothpaste, shoe polish, and cigarettes. They also sold liquor, radios, televisions, expensive stereo equipment, diamonds, and furs. Additionally, exchange concessionaires who sold diamonds, furs, silks, watches, leather goods, and other luxury items had virtually unlimited duty-free import privileges.[22] The Saigon government maintained that many of these tax-free items were being sold to Vietnamese citizens, violating Vietnamese customs and commerce laws, fueling inflation, and injuring legitimate Vietnamese businessmen. The Irregular Practices Committee not only investigated Vietnamese allegations of black-marketing, but also formulated corrective action to curb it and related criminal misconduct.[23]

Based on the committee's recommendations, the U.S. ambassador directed the implementation of an automated system for recording dollar conversions and purchases, which led to more stringent inspections of exchange concessionaire goods. MACV also identified civilian abusers of military privileges and revoked their privilege cards. MACV judge advocates assisted in promulgating new directives identifying activities prohibited for U.S. military and civilian personnel, contractors doing business in Vietnam at the invitation of the United States, and all persons authorized to use exchanges, clubs, post offices, and other U.S. military facilities. As illegal currency transactions often went along with black market commodity sales, MACV lawyers also provided advice concerning the Military Payment Certificate program. After 1 September 1965, U.S. dollars were no longer negotiable at U.S. facilities, and Americans were forbidden to bring dollars into Vietnam.[24] Rather, all U.S. troops were paid in Military Pay Certificates, or "scrip," which allowed U.S. dollars to be withdrawn from the Vietnamese economy. Scrip, printed by the United States and as freely negotiable as dollars, was used at all U.S. facilities. Its use curbed illegal currency transactions because scrip could not easily be converted into U.S. currency and because only authorized personnel were permitted to hold scrip. The goal was to separate the U.S. and Vietnamese monetary systems. This aim, however, was only partially successful; Military Payment Certificates issued in 1965 were replaced in 1968 and replaced again in 1969.

Although the Irregular Practices Committee's original purpose was to suppress black-marketeering, currency manipulation, and related misconduct, the group's composition naturally made it a clearinghouse for a variety of policy issues. Thus, by 1970, the committee was examining tax evasion by U.S. and Vietnamese nationals and the appropriateness of exercising military criminal jurisdiction over U.S. civilians and generally coordinating anticorruption efforts. It also served as a point of contact for Saigon government officials seeking assistance in criminal and civil matters. For example, in June and July 1970, the committee and Col. Lawrence H. Williams, the MACV staff judge advocate, considered a request from the Vietnamese Ministry of Finance for a list of all Vietnamese subcontractors or persons hired by U.S. contractors to determine whether these contractors were reporting income. They also responded to a Vietnamese complaint that civilian contractors with no U.S. government affiliation were being allowed on MACV charter flights and Air America flights and discussed assistance to the Vietnamese to repatriate third country national undesirables.[25]

Setting uniform criteria for reporting, investigating, processing, and supervising claims in Vietnam was the last major area in which MACV judge advocates formulated legal policy. The buildup of troops and materiel from 1965 to 1969 meant an increase in claims for compensation, and MACV lawyers designed and implemented a well-organized and well-administered indemnification program to compensate for losses resulting from U.S. government activity. This promoted two important policy goals. First, fair and timely restitution showed the Vietnamese that the U.S. government was interested in justice and the welfare of Vietnamese citizens. Second, an effective claims program supported the war against the guerrillas. Col. Prugh, MACV staff judge advocate from 1964 to 1966, believed strongly that a well-run claims program was one way to "create a climate favorable to respect for law and order." If the Vietnamese people saw that the law conferred a benefit in compensating them for injuries caused by the U.S. government, they would respect both the law and the government that made it.[26]

Lt. Col. George R. Robinson, MACV claims judge advocate from November 1964 to November 1965, was chiefly responsible for implementing a fast and fair claims service during the early months of the U.S. buildup. With division-level judge advocate service prior to arriving in Vietnam, Robinson was an experienced officer. Consequently, as new U.S. combat units arrived in Vietnam, Robinson visited them to explain claims processing procedures, basic Vietnamese government structure, and sources of aid for those injured by combat action. In early 1965, Robinson spearheaded the revision of MACV Directive 25-1, *Claims*, which governed the payment of claims for noncombat damage. When reissued in May 1965, the new directive was easier for nonlawyer unit claims officers to follow and included trilingual (English, Vietnamese, and Chinese) claims forms and a sample letter of condolence, in both English and Vietnamese, for use in making a solatia payment. Such a payment or gift indicates sympathy or compassion for serious personal injury or death, and MACV headquarters encouraged unit claims officers to make it. As a result, a solatium of value not exceeding $20, accompanied by the letter found in MACV Directive 25-1, would be routinely made by a unit's claims officer in appropriate situations. Of course, the aggrieved party eventually would file a claim and receive compensation for any personal injury or loss. Until that claim was paid, however, the small solatia payment was a tangible demonstration of official U.S. sympathy for the South Vietnamese victim. Providing for solatia payments also showed how the law could be used to enhance the Army's image among the local population, thus furthering the overall policy goal of winning "hearts and minds."[27]

The more difficult policy issue was the payment of combat-related claims. Traditionally, the host country is responsible for such claims but, at least initially, the Republic of Vietnam had no program to compensate its citizens for injuries or damage suffered in combat situations. In August 1965, for example, a U.S. Air Force B-57 bomber returning from a combat mission crashed in the city of Nha Trang, killing a number of civilians and destroying a great deal of property. Viet Cong radio broadcasts accused the United States of criminal recklessness, and this generated much bad feeling toward Americans. Lt. Col. Robinson flew immediately to Nha Trang with two other members of the MACV staff judge advocate's office and began accepting claims from Vietnamese civilians. While Robinson was processing claims, however, an announcement from the Pentagon stated that no compensation for this disaster could be paid because damage resulting directly or indirectly from combat was not permitted under the Foreign Claims Act. Robinson and Col. Prugh, however, convinced MACV headquarters that payments to claimants would gain the goodwill of the people. First, it would demonstrate to the Vietnamese that a government can view itself as responsible for its bad acts. Second, it would show that a person has a right to pursue a claim for injury against the government, a concept alien to Vietnamese culture. The result was that Defense Department contingency funds were used to pay these claims. Similar claims situations resulted in MACV's recommending that the Foreign Claims Act be amended to allow payment of certain claims indirectly related to the combat activities of U.S. forces, and Congress made such a change to the law in 1968. As a result, claims filed after this date were payable if they arose out of a military aircraft accident or malfunction that was indirectly related to combat and occurred while the aircraft was preparing for, going to, or returning from a combat mission. Consequently, claims like those Robinson had handled in Nha Trang in August 1965 could now be paid.[28]

MACV Advisory Program

Believing that "a successful counterinsurgency program" required respect for law and order, and that developing such respect "would

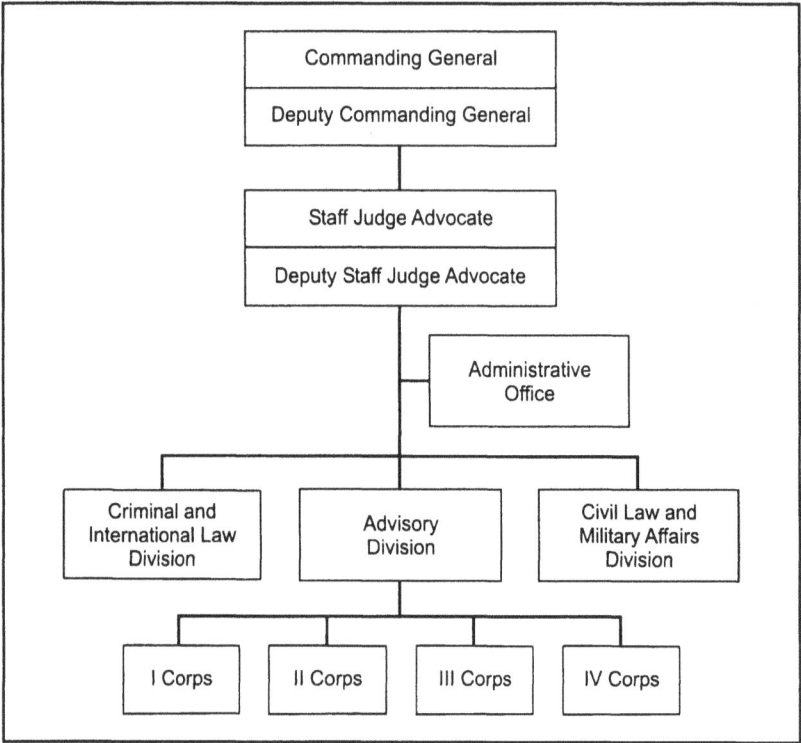

Figure 2. Organization of MACV Office of Staff Judge Advocate (1967)

increase the efficiency of the armed forces, deter subversive activities . . . and promote loyalty to the Saigon government," the MACV staff judge advocate established an Advisory Branch in July 1965.[29] Using the law and lawyers to further the allied mission in Vietnam was a unique approach, and by late 1965 the work done by the Advisory Branch accounted for roughly 40 percent of the MACV staff judge advocate total workload.[30]

At the Saigon level, the advisory effort was aimed at the Directorate of Military Justice and other Vietnamese government agencies and focused on improving such matters as budgeting, desertion control, tables of organization and equipment, and administration of the court and prison systems. But MACV lawyers also participated in nongovernmental activities in Saigon as a way of informally influencing Vietnamese lawyers, government officials, and other policymakers. To strengthen his personal relationship with the Public Prosecutor of Saigon, Col. Prugh taught him English two nights a week.

Prugh also made contact with future Vietnamese lawyers when he continued teaching the American jurisprudence classes started by MAAG lawyers a few years earlier at the University of Saigon.[31] Finally, Prugh organized the Law Society of Free Vietnam as a way to foster personal associations and to expose the Vietnamese to "new alternatives for dealing with legal problems," with a view toward improving their own legal institutions. Beginning with an evening meeting on 5 May 1965, the Law Society held a series of meetings for all Vietnamese lawyers, judges, law students, government officials, and interested army officers, presenting "a sampling of American legal ideas and attitudes to an influential segment of Vietnamese society in a manner the Vietnamese could accept without resentment." The first meeting opened with a brief introductory talk titled "The Citizen's Role in Law," followed by a question and answer session. Later Law Society meetings featured panel discussions, mixed team debates, selected motion pictures, and individual presentations on topics such as "Trial by Jury" and "Judicial Review Procedures." Initially, the Law Society of Free Vietnam drew large and interested audiences from the Vietnamese and American legal communities. As the war heated up, however, it became increasingly difficult to assemble the society, raising questions about its long-term impact.[32]

Outside Saigon, the Advisory Division's field advisers, located in each of the four corps areas, were the eyes and ears of the MACV staff judge advocate, monitoring military discipline in South Vietnamese units, the effectiveness of resources control, and the functioning of South Vietnamese military courts and prisons.[33] No two field advisers had the same approach to their role, and activities varied according to location and "to a great extent on the relationship between the military lawyer and the U.S. commander for whom he worked."[34] Both I and II Corps had field advisers from August 1965 until March 1973. On the other hand, III Corps, centered on Saigon, and IV Corps, in the Mekong Delta, had field advisers only intermittently for this period. Initially, the field adviser in I Corps, the northernmost and farthest area from Saigon, was located in Hue; after the Tet offensive of 1968, he moved to Da Nang, when the Vietnamese military courts and prison moved there. The II Corps adviser served in the largest corps area, comprising coastal and highlands provinces. On the other hand, the III Corps adviser stayed in Saigon where his work differed from the other advisers in that he taught law courses at the University of Saigon law school.

The experiences of Capt. John T. Sherwood, first judge advocate field adviser for II Corps, illustrate these advisers' varied work. It was

Col. George S. Prugh, right, MACV staff judge advocate, presents the Air Medal to Capt. John T. Sherwood, Jr., April 1966. Prugh established a unique advisory program in which Army lawyers like Sherwood advised their Vietnamese counterparts on ways to improve their legal facilities and programs.

shortly after Sherwood arrived in Nha Trang that the U.S. B-57 crashed there. Sherwood spent several days with a committee of Vietnamese citizens inspecting the damage to determine an equitable monetary settlement. In addition, he conferred with the Nha Trang provost marshal about the conduct of some members of the National Police who were ineffective in preventing looting after the crash. And he negotiated with a French-owned electric company in the city concerning liability for property damage arising out of the incident. Sherwood also traveled extensively during the time he served as field adviser, from August 1965 to May 1966. In the two-month period of August and September 1965, he taught military justice to Vietnamese Regional Forces and Popular Forces in Qui Nhon; visited the Vietnamese Military Academy, Command and General Staff College, and U.S. Operations Mission province representative in Da Lat; and attended an oath of allegiance ceremony at Ban Me Thuot in which 300 dissident Montagnards pledged fealty to the Saigon government. Sherwood also inspected Regional Forces and Popular Forces training at Tuy Hoa, observed pacification efforts in Phu Yen Province and, after conferring with the U.S. command on military justice matters, redrafted a provost marshal directive on confiscating Military Payment

Certificates from Vietnamese employees of U.S. installations. In addition to advising, Sherwood reviewed a treatise on Vietnamese law written in English by a Vietnamese military lawyer and represented two U.S. soldiers charged with rape, attempted rape, robbery, and assault at a pretrial investigation. He also traveled to Bangkok to discuss the legal status of U.S. personnel visiting Thailand and the feasibility of a legal advisory program in that country. Finally, he made three parachute jumps with the first Montagnards ever to be trained for airborne operations and did a detailed study of the methods used by U.S. units in II Corps for handling captured enemy personnel.[35]

Lawyering at U.S. Army, Vietnam

The mission of the USARV staff judge advocate was to provide full legal services for the USARV commander, deputy commander, and staff, as well as for all major subordinate commanders as needed. The USARV staff judge advocate also "exercised staff supervision over all judge advocate activities in the U.S. Army, Vietnam."[36] This meant

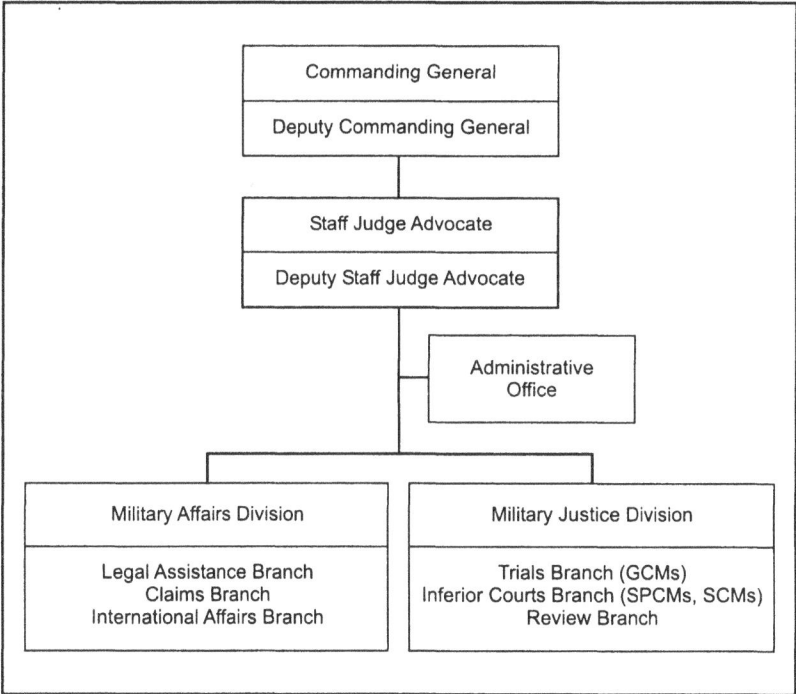

Figure 3. Legal Organization of USARV Ofice of Staff Judge Advocate (December 1967).

that he monitored legal operations in all Army organizations in Vietnam, providing guidance and assistance. As a practical matter, the staff judge advocate at USARV also acted as a higher headquarters for personnel and other administrative matters relating to Army lawyers in Vietnam.

Organization of Legal Services at U.S. Army, Vietnam

When organized in 1965, the USARV staff judge advocate's office had five military lawyers-one colonel, two majors, and two captains. It expanded rapidly, however, and between 1966 and 1969, there were no fewer than ten lawyers in the headquarters office. Initially, the operation was divided into two sections. A Military Affairs Division, with Legal Assistance, Claims, and International Affairs Branches, handled all noncriminal legal matters. A Military Justice Division, with Trial, Inferior Courts, and Review Branches, provided all criminal law support. This two-part framework had been the norm for staff judge advocate operations since World War II. But when Col. John Jay Douglass replaced Col. William B. Carne as USARV staff judge advocate in July 1968, Douglass decided that this traditional way of

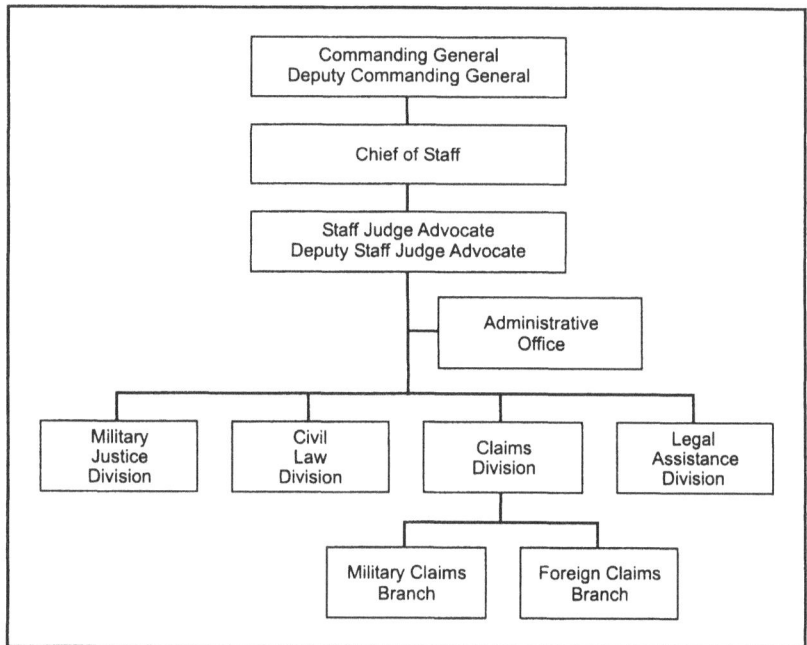

Figure 4. Legal Organization of USARV Office of Staff Judge Advocate (September 1968).

providing services was no longer suitable because "it didn't reflect how legal work was being done" at USARV. For example, the Military Affairs Division, located at USARV headquarters at Long Binh, was responsible for all claims activities in Vietnam. Yet its foreign claims operation, with its downtown Saigon location, operated with great autonomy. So it made sense to remove the claims function from the Military Affairs Division and establish a separate Claims Division. Once claims were removed, it was a short step to removing legal assistance as well. As Douglass later noted, this new system was the same one he had used while serving as staff judge advocate at Fort Riley, Kansas.[37]

The new office at USARV headquarters had four divisions-Military Justice, Civil Law, Claims, and Legal Assistance. The Military Justice Division prosecuted and defended all general courts-martial and advised nonlawyers prosecuting and defending special courts-martial. After the enactment of the Military Justice Act in 1968, the division expanded to provide lawyers as trial and defense counsel in special courts-martial. USARV judge advocates practicing criminal law also arranged for the attendance of witnesses from all courts-martial jurisdictions in Vietnam when these were required in the United States

Judge Advocate General Maj. General Kenneth D. Hodson, center, visits Vietnam in November 1968. With him are, left to right, Col. Thomas H. Reese, Staff Judge Advocate, 1st Logistical Command; Col. John J. Douglass, Staff Judge Advocate, USARV; Lt. Col. Robert Clarke, Chief, Personnel, Plans & Training Office, Office of the Judge Advocate General; and Col. Paul Tobin, Military Judge, U.S. Army Trial Judiciary, Vietnam.

or for attendance at other foreign trials. The USARV Civil Law Division interpreted and advised on the applicability of laws, regulations, and directives concerning the status of military and civilian members in noncriminal matters. It also reviewed investigations concerning the post exchange system, clubs, messes, security violations, postal losses, reports of survey, elimination boards, and collateral investigations involving aircraft accidents. It also advised on procurement matters and real estate and provided counsel for respondents before administrative elimination boards. The Claims Division, subdivided further into military personnel claims and foreign claims branches, adjudicated all military personnel claims filed by soldiers, sailors, airmen, and Marines and all foreign claims filed by Vietnamese and other foreign nationals. Finally, the Legal Assistance Division offered the full range of legal advice to individual soldiers. Supporting Douglass and the twelve military attorneys on his staff were one warrant officer, seven enlisted personnel, one civilian court reporter, and one Vietnamese translator-interpreter.

From 1965 to 1969 about sixty judge advocates served at USARV headquarters. Staff judge advocates during those years were Cols. Dean R. Dort (1965-1966), Hal H. Bookout (1966-1967), William B. Carne (1967-1968), Douglass (1968-1969), and Wilton B. Persons, Jr. (1969-1970). Persons later served as the Judge Advocate General from

USARV staff judge advocate's office at Long Binh, July 1968. While the hours were long, the facilities at USARV were not much different from those in stateside Army legal offices.

1975 to 1979. Other notables serving at USARV during this period were Lt. Col. Lloyd K. Rector and Maj. John L. Fugh. Rector later served as a judge advocate brigadier general and Fugh was the Judge Advocate General from 1991 to 1993. Additionally, many lawyers who were not members of the Judge Advocate General's Corps joined the corps in practicing law in Vietnam. A number of licensed attorneys had been drafted and were serving in the enlisted ranks. These men often became legal clerks and, as the demand for lawyers increased, eventually practiced law as legal assistance officers. More than a few licensed lawyers also served in Vietnam in other Army branches such as the Transportation Corps or Adjutant General's Corps. Unlike the Judge Advocate General's Corps, which required a four-year commitment, other Army branches had a two-year obligation. Many lawyers with Reserve Officer Training Corps obligations chose the two-year route, hoping that they would serve their two-year obligation in Europe or in the United States. When these non-Judge Advocate General's Corps lawyers arrived in Vietnam, however, they discovered that judge advocates needed their legal skills, particularly after the Military Justice Act of 1968 took effect on 1 September 1969. For his part, Col. Persons asked the USARV G1 to detail all incoming licensed attorneys to his headquarters office. These non-judge advocate lawyers were then distributed as needed to Army units in Vietnam.

Military Justice

More than anything else, practicing law at USARV, particularly after passage of the Military Justice Act in 1968, meant prosecuting and defending courts-martial. When Congress replaced the separate Army and Navy court-martial systems with a "uniform" code of military law in 1950, it required that courts-martial mirror, "so far as . . . practicable," civilian criminal trials in U.S. district courts. A decade later, Senator Samuel J. Ervin of North Carolina and other reformers went further, criticizing "legal decisionmaking by laymen" in the military justice system and calling for lawyer involvement at courts-martial.[38]

Satisfied with the status quo, the services initially resisted. By 1968, however, opposition had softened and, with the support of Army Judge Advocate General Maj. Gen. Kenneth J. Hodson, Congress enacted far-reaching changes through the Military Justice Act.[39] Chief among them was creation of the military judge position, replacing the "law officer," and giving the new position duties and powers similar to those of a civilian judge. These included the power to try a case "by military judge alone," the authority to call a court into session without the attendance of the members for the purpose of disposing with various motions, ruling on pertinent legal matters, and arraigning the accused. All of these issues had previously been decided by the panel members. The independence of the new military judge position was strengthened by the act's requirement that military judges be appointed from a field judiciary under the command of the Judge Advocate General. Although the Army had previously created a field judiciary without this legislative basis, the new act required the presiding judge to be independent of the convening authority whereas, before, the law officer could have been a member of the accused's unit and thus subject to the same commander. Finally, the independence of military judges was made even more apparent by regulations allowing them to wear robes and to be addressed as "Your Honor."[40]

Maj. Gen. Kenneth J. Hodson, the first Judge Advocate General to visit Vietnam. Hodson was the principal architect of the Military Justice Act of 1968, which revolutionized the practice of military justice in the Armed Forces.

The second major change to the Uniform Code was the new role of lawyers at special courts-martial. The amendment did not require lawyers at this level of court, but it did provide that the accused was to "be afforded the opportunity to be represented" by a lawyer "unless counsel having such qualifications cannot be obtained on account of physical conditions or military exigencies." Additionally, the 1968 act prohibited the imposition of a punitive discharge at a special court-martial unless a lawyer counsel defended the accused and a military judge was detailed to the court. Commanders who had long considered special courts as courts of discipline over which they exercised considerable control as convening authorities discovered not only that the rule of law now favored justice over discipline but also that their control had been greatly reduced.[41]

The implementation of the Military Justice Act required more lawyers to serve as counsel and more lawyers to serve as judges. But just how many attorneys? The Judge Advocate General advised the

50

Army Staff that 401 new lawyers were needed. Apparently, this number was arrived at based on an estimate that 400 new attorneys were needed, with one added to give legitimacy. That is, knowing that the round number 400 would be viewed with suspicion, the number 401 was presented as the needed number.[42] Implementing the new changes to the code also required a new Manual for Court-Martial, and the 1969 revised edition was published in time for the 1 September 1969 effective date of the new act. Finally, the need for special court-martial judges resulted in the addition of both full-time and part-time judges as well as the establishment of a supervisory judge program.

Implementing the Military Justice Act brought particular challenges for USARV judge advocates practicing criminal law. Prior to the effective date of the Military Justice Act, the Uniform Code had been interpreted to give virtually every battalion commander the authority to convene a special court-martial. To promote uniformity and better manage legal assets, both Col. Douglass and Col. Persons tried consolidating special courts-martial at the brigade level. They were mostly successful, but the 1st and 4th Infantry Divisions "held out to the bitter end" and declined to follow their guidance.[43] Second, Douglass and Persons had supervisory responsibility for some thirteen general court-martial jurisdictions, and the new Military Justice Act meant a huge influx of new attorneys. Handling so many convening authorities, and the cases generated by them, was a tremendous workload. Finally, although U.S. units continued offensive operations, the political commitment had been made to begin withdrawing American units from Vietnam. As a result, the third challenge facing USARV judge advocates was taking responsibility to "clean up" remaining cases. For example, the 9th Infantry Division was going home in 1969, and all its cases-some tried, some tried but not transcribed, some tried and transcribed but still needing a posttrial review and convening authority action-had to be taken over by another jurisdiction. The USARV staff judge advocates and their lawyers were responsible for ensuring the orderly "hand off" of military justice actions from departing units to the U.S. forces remaining in Vietnam.[44]

U.S. Army, Vietnam, and its subordinate units tried roughly 25,000 courts-martial between 1965 and 1969. There were 9,922 courts-martial in Vietnam in 1969, at the peak of the U.S. buildup, of which 377 were general courts, 7,314 were special courts, and 2,231 were summary courts. Similarly, a large number of Article 15s were administered in Vietnam between the years 1965 and 1969—66,702 in 1969 alone. Of the thousands of courts-martial, a large number were for such military offenses as absence without leave, disobedience of orders, and misbehavior of a sentinel. Some were prosecutions for assault and for larceny. Although there were few illegal drug prosecutions in 1966, a continued rise in the drug-use rate by U.S. troops translated into more and more criminal prosecutions. By 1967, marijuana cigarettes were selling for twenty cents each in Saigon and one dollar each in Da Nang. Opium was one dollar per injection, and morphine five dollars per vial. The result was that by 1969 roughly 20 percent of the special courts tried in Vietnam were for drug-related offenses.[45]

Two of the best known criminal incidents occurring between 1965 and 1969 were the killing of Vietnamese civilians by soldiers at My Lai in 1968 and the murder of an alleged enemy agent by Special Forces troops near Nha Trang in 1969. On 16 March 1968, members of Company C, 1st Battalion, 20th Infantry, an element of the Americal Division, murdered some 350 innocent Vietnamese civilians at the small village of My Lai in southern I Corps. Outside of the division there was no official knowledge of the atrocity until April 1969, when a veteran who had heard of the killings wrote to Gen. Westmoreland, then Army chief of staff, describing his suspicions and requesting an inquiry. The Army's Criminal Investigation Division determined that 1st Lt. William L. Calley and twelve men under his command were chiefly responsible for the killings. In September 1969, Calley was charged with the murder of 109 Vietnamese civilians, and in November that same year, a second soldier, S.Sgt. David Mitchell, was charged with multiple counts of murder and assault with intent to commit murder. Eleven other soldiers were also charged with murder.[46]

Of the thirteen men charged, only Calley was convicted. Proceedings against six accused were dismissed for insufficient evidence. The rest were tried by court-martial and found not guilty. The first court-martial proceeding was against S.Sgt. Mitchell. The military judge was Lt. Col. Robinson, who had served as MACV claims judge advocate from 1964 to 1965. In a controversial decision, Robinson ruled that four prosecution witnesses would not be permitted to testify unless the defense received access to their previous testimony before a U.S. House of Representatives subcommittee investigating the My Lai atrocity. When the congressman running the subcommittee refused to release relevant testimony, the prosecutor in the Mitchell court-martial no longer had any witnesses who could testify with certainty that Mitchell had killed civilians at My Lai. The jury acquitted Mitchell of all charges.[47]

The courtroom at the 23rd Infantry Division (Americal), Chu Lai, 1970. Nothing could be more utilitarian in design or appearance.

Of the twelve Americal Division officers accused of covering up the atrocity, only Calley's company commander, Capt. Ernest L. Medina, and his brigade commander, Col. Oran K. Henderson, ever came to trial. Both were court-martialed and both were acquitted. Charges against Gen. Koster, the division commander, for failing to report the killings to MACV headquarters were also were dismissed. Secretary of the Army Stanley R. Resor, however, punished Koster administratively by demoting him from major general to his permanent grade of brigadier general and revoking his award of the Distinguished Service Medal.[48] On 29 March 1971, Calley was found guilty of premeditated murder by a general court-martial convened at Fort Benning, Georgia, and was sentenced to life imprisonment. Three days later, the White House interfered in the judicial process by announcing that President Richard M. Nixon would personally review Calley's case before the sentence took effect and that, in the interim, Calley would be under house arrest. On 20 August 1971, the commanding general, Third United States Army, took action as the general court-martial convening authority. He approved the findings of premeditated murder against Calley, but reduced his sentence to twenty years' confinement. In April 1974, after both the Army Court of Military Review and the U.S. Court of Military Appeals had rejected Calley's appeals and had affirmed the findings and sentence, the new Secretary of the Army, Howard H.

Callaway, reduced his sentence further to ten years. This made Calley eligible for parole after six months and, after serving a short time in jail at Fort Leavenworth, Kansas, Calley was paroled in November 1974.[49]

While the war crimes committed at My Lai caused much consternation and soul-searching among Americans generally, the ramifications of this tragedy on the Army were just as far-reaching. The Peers Inquiry, so-named because its senior member was Lt. Gen. William R. Peers, thoroughly investigated the murders. Peers and his team examined the causes of the incident, the thirty individuals involved, and the subsequent cover-up at the Americal Division. For Army lawyers, the Peers Report finding with the most significant legal ramification was the determination that inadequate training in the Law of War was a contributory cause of the killings. Particularly damning was the report's finding that Law of War training in Calley's unit was deficient in regards to the proper treatment of civilians and the responsibility for reporting war crimes.

Almost immediately, senior members of the Judge Advocate General's Corps began looking for ways to correct this deficiency. In May 1970, the regulation governing Law of War training was revised so that soldiers received more thorough instruction in the Hague and Geneva Conventions. Significantly, the revised regulation required that instruction be presented by judge advocates "together with officers with command experience preferably in combat." This ensured that the training had a firm grounding in real-world experience while also demonstrating that instruction in the conventions was a command responsibility.

Of greater importance was the initiative taken by retired Col. Waldemar A. Solf. In 1972, while serving as the chief of the International Affairs Division at the Office of the Judge Advocate General, Solf suggested that the Army propose to the Defense Department that it create a DoD-level Law of War program. This idea was wholeheartedly endorsed by Gen. Prugh, who was then serving as the Judge Advocate General. As a result of Solf's recommendation, DoD Directive 5100.77, promulgated by the secretary of defense on 5 November 1974, not only established a unified Law of War program for the armed forces, but also made the Army Judge Advocate General's Corps the lead organization in implementing it.[50]

In the so-called Green Beret Affair, members of the U.S. Army Special Forces allegedly murdered a South Vietnamese double agent named Thai Khac Chuyen in June 1969. The New York Times reported that the killing had been done at the suggestion of a Central Intelligence

Defense counsel in the "Green Beret Affair," in which Special Forces personnel were accused of murdering a South Vietnamese double agent, 1969. After the *New York Times* reported that the killing had been done at the suggestion of a CIA agent, there was considerable public interest in the case. From left to right: Capt. J. William Hart, XXIV Corps; Capt. Myron D. Stutzman, USARV; and Capt. J. Stevens Berry, II Field Force.

Agency agent in Nha Trang. The investigation into the murder implicated the commander of the 5th Special Forces Group, Col. Robert B. Rheault, and seven members of his command.[51] Angry that American soldiers had taken the law into their own hands, and believing that Rheault had lied to him, Gen. Creighton W. Abrams, the MACV commander, expressed a desire to have MACV prosecute the case. Col. Bruce C. Babbitt, the MACV staff judge advocate, however, convinced Abrams that court-martial proceedings were the service component's rather than the unified command's responsibility. USARV, Babbitt advised, should conduct the investigation and decide whether criminal trials were warranted.[52] As USARV judge advocates and Army investigators gathered evidence in the case, the Central Intelligence Agency was uncooperative. It denied any involvement in the murder but also refused to provide classified documents about Special Forces operations in Vietnam requested by the defense lawyers. Recognizing that publicity could only assist their Special Forces clients, both the military and civilian defense attorneys issued press releases and gave interviews. Capt. J. Stevens Berry, a II Field Force judge advocate defending one of the Special Forces officers, appeared on network television two nights running, alleging that the government's refusal to give him access to classified documents was harming the defense and that the Army's prosecution of "those gallant men" was motivated by Abrams' anger rather than justice. Members of Congress were sharply critical of the Army's actions. Congressman Peter W. Rodino of New Jersey called the prosecution "one of the weirdest—and probably cruelest—trials in the military history of this nation."[53] When the Central Intelligence Agency, with the approval of President Nixon, refused for the final time to cooperate in the investigation, Secretary Resor decided that a fair trial would be impossible. He yielded to the wishes of Secretary of Defense Melvin R. Laird, Gen. Westmoreland, and others in dismissing all charges against Rheault and the other soldiers.[54]

Civil Law and Claims

The Civil Law Division prepared opinions and advised on the interpretation and application of laws, regulations, and directives. Subjects handled by the division included issues involving the status of USARV military and civilian personnel (except criminal matters), military security, operations, logistics, and civil affairs. Lawyers in the Civil Law Division reviewed for legal sufficiency investigations concerning post exchanges, clubs and messes, security violations, and postal losses; reports of survey; elimination boards; and collateral investigations involving aircraft accidents. The division also arranged for the travel of soldiers from Vietnam to the United States when these persons were needed as witnesses in U.S. legal proceedings, issued legal opinions on international law, and monitored Geneva Conventions lectures to USARV troops. It provided counsel for respondents at administrative elimination boards and advised on procurement law matters. Finally, the Civil Law Division was also the focal point for inquiries from the Litigation Division of the Judge Advocate General's Office in the Pentagon. In February 1969 for example, the division compiled an investigative report in connection with a lawsuit filed by United Fruit Company against the United States. The U.S. Army had chartered a United Fruit ship to transport cargo to Vietnam. When the ship arrived at Qui Nhon in December 1966, an Army tugboat collided with the ship, causing damage in the amount of $32,000. United Fruit sued the United States for this loss, and the Civil Law Division provided the investigative report needed to defend against the suit or settle it.[55] Similarly, in November 1969 the division was asked by the Litigation Division in Washington to locate the 173d Airborne Brigade's daily staff journal or pertinent unit history for 31 July 1968. While on patrol, a sergeant in the unit, Donald W. Morrison, discovered $150,000 in a container in an unoccupied underground cave. He turned the money over to his company commander, but later asked that it be returned to him. His request was refused. Having since left Vietnam and been discharged from the Army, Morrison sued the United States for the return of "his" money. Apparently, the Civil Law Division located the requested information. Morrison's suit, however, was dismissed by the U.S. district court since abandoned property found by a soldier during combat operations becomes the property of the United States.[56]

The Army had single-service responsibility for processing claims in favor of or against U.S. forces in Vietnam. As MACV had ceased its claims processing by 1966, USARV judge advocates were solely responsible for administering a claims program in Vietnam. The number of claims for damaged or destroyed possessions, equipment, and clothing grew rapidly as the Viet Cong and North Vietnamese stepped up their attacks on U.S. forces and as American operations intensified. Similarly, the buildup of American forces in Vietnam brought with it increased claims by Vietnamese nationals for personal injury and property damage. The impact of heavy military truck traffic on a people accustomed to the bicycle, small car, and animal-drawn wagons easily led to traffic chaos and many claims.[57] By the end of 1969 the number of claims filed and the resulting backlog were significant.

The USARV commander had authority to create two foreign claims commissions with a monetary jurisdiction up to $15,000 each and twelve one-man commissions with a monetary jurisdiction up to $1,000 each. An award in excess of $5,000 was subject to approval by the appointing authority, and the USARV staff judge advocate was delegated by the USARV commander to act for him in claims matters.[58]

Although USARV legal operations were located at Long Binh, the Foreign Claims Division was housed across the street from the National Assembly building in downtown Saigon. This greatly increased access for Vietnamese claimants and meant that the USARV claims judge advocates were located near their Saigon counterparts. As claims resulting from combat activities were handled by the Vietnamese under the Military Civic Action Program while the USARV Foreign Claims Division paid noncombat-related claims, a close working relationship developed between the Vietnamese and Americans. Forms and procedures, modeled somewhat along the lines of the U.S. noncombat claims program but less formal and more streamlined, were

Lt. Col. James D. Clause (far left), MACV SJA Advisory Division, and Maj. Leonard G. Crowley (far right), USARV SJA Foreign Claims Division, receive the Vietnamese Justice Medal (Second Class) from Minister of Justice Le Van Thu (second from left) in Saigon ceremonies in 1970. The decoration was Vietnam's highest judicial honor for foreigners; only a few judge advocates received it.

implemented by the Vietnamese for the payment of claims that the USARV judge advocates could not handle. The line between combat and noncombat claims was often difficult to draw, but since in almost every case there were innocent victims needing relief, the Vietnamese and Americans worked together so that compensation was available regardless of cause.[59]

Maj. Leonard G. Crowley's experiences illustrate claims work done by USARV. Crowley, one of a handful of judge advocates to serve two twelve-month tours in Vietnam, was chief of the USARV Foreign Claims Division during his first tour from March 1969 to April 1970. With responsibility for handling all tort claims by foreign nationals against U.S. military forces in Vietnam, Crowley had four captains assisting him in downtown Saigon, where he had his office. Additionally, one captain under his supervision ran a satellite claims program in Da Nang. Crowley also managed thirty-five U.S. military and Vietnamese civilian clerks and translators.

Most of the noncombat claims were for damage arising out of traffic accidents, often involving collisions between 2 1/2-ton or "deuce and a half" trucks and motorbikes, bicycles, or pedestrians. Although most of

58

the claims were for negligent acts committed by U.S. forces, Crowley's operation paid claims for intentional acts, too. A farmer would be paid the Vietnamese piaster equivalent of $1,000 for his dead male water buffalo if it had been used for target practice by soldiers passing by on patrol. This amount, roughly equivalent to the amount paid for wrongful death of a woman or child, was increased if the dead water buffalo was a female carrying a calf. If the farmer butchered the water buffalo and ate it, then USARV claims judge advocates deducted salvage value from the monies paid.[60]

One of the most interesting claims handled by the USARV Foreign Claims Division during this period involved the Green Beret Affair. While criminal action was pending against Col. Rheault, the widow of the victim appeared at Maj. Crowley's office, accompanied by her Vietnamese attorney. The dead man's employment contract provided that if he was missing for more than sixty days in connection with his duties, he was presumed to be dead and a death gratuity equal to one year's salary was payable to his next of kin. His widow now sought these monies. The victim's body, which had apparently been disposed of at sea, was never located, and the Special Forces command admitted no complicity. After having the widow sign a release absolving the United States of further liability for the death of her husband, Major Crowley personally delivered $6,472 in piasters to her-three times her missing husband's salary. The widow later filed a much larger wrongful death claim against the United States but, as Crowley had made the widow's attorney sign his name as a witness on the release form before paying her the gratuity, this rebutted her claim that she had not understood the significance of signing a release.[61]

Lawyering in the Field

Each major combat and support unit had its own legal staff. At the beginning of the intervention, the Army's Table of Organization and Equipment authorized five lawyers in a division: one lieutenant colonel, two majors, and two captains. A division deployed in Vietnam, however, might be overstrength one or more judge advocates. Additionally, non-judge advocate attorneys often supplemented a staff judge advocate's operations, particularly after the passage of the Military Justice Act in 1968, when more lawyers were needed. For example, although the 1st Cavalry Division was authorized only five attorneys, its staff judge advocate had some fifteen attorneys in 1969, roughly half of whom were not members of the Judge Advocate General's Corps.[62]

From 1965 to 1969 more than 350 judge advocates served at units other than Headquarters, MACV, and Headquarters, USARV. Combat units with assigned military lawyers included: 173d Airborne Brigade; 196th and 199th Infantry Brigades (Light); 1st Brigade, 5th Infantry Division (Mechanized); 5th Special Forces Group; Task Force OREGON; 1st, 4th, 9th, 23d, and 25th Infantry Divisions; 1st Cavalry Division (Airmobile); 3d Brigade, 82d Airborne Division; 101st Airborne Division; XXIV Corps; and I and II Field Forces, Vietnam.

Support units with assigned judge advocates included: 1st Logistical Command and its four support commands; 1st Aviation Brigade; 1st Signal Brigade; 29th Civil Affairs Company; 525th Military Intelligence Group; 124th and 125th Transportation Commands; The Support Troops, Vietnam; U.S. Army Engineer Command and U.S. Army Engineer Troops (Provisional); and U.S. Army Procurement Agency.

The experiences of Army lawyers at the 173d Airborne Brigade, II Field Force, 1st Logistical Command, 101st Airborne Division, and U.S. Army Trial Judiciary, Vietnam, illustrate lawyering "in the field" from 1965 to 1969.

173d Airborne Brigade

This 5,000-man independent brigade arrived in III Corps from Okinawa in May 1965, commanded by Brig. Gen. Ellis W. Williamson. Accompanying it were two judge advocates, Capts. Raymond C. McRorie and Charles A. White, Jr. Over the next year, they provided the legal advice and support needed by the command group and the brigade's soldiers, including legal assistance, claims, and military justice. Living and working conditions were Spartan. Capts. McRorie and White shared a General Purpose, Medium, tent. This heavy olive-drab canvas structure, approximately 30 feet long and 15 feet wide, was designed to sleep twenty soldiers or so. McRorie and White, however, used their tent differently: they slept on cots in the middle third of the tent and set up their office in the front third. The courtroom was in the back third.

The 173d Airborne convened only special courts-martial, and Gen. Williamson appointed two court panels. One remained at brigade headquarters at Bien Hoa Air Base to handle discipline in the rear. The other was with the forward-deployed brigade elements farther north. Misconduct ranged from aggravated assault and drunkenness to disobedience of orders and absence without leave. Punishments usually were forfeitures and reductions, as a sentence to confinement meant the soldier had to be shipped to the stockade in Okinawa. As some viewed returning to Okinawa—even to the stockade—as preferable to conditions in Vietnam, most sentences did not include confinement. Under the Uniform Code of Military Justice at the time, lawyer participation in special courts was not required. This meant that Capt. McRorie advised the president of the court and the nonlawyer prosecutor on court procedure and military law. Capt. White counseled the nonlawyer defense counsel. Similarly, when nonjudicial punishment was administered under Article 15, McRorie counseled the command and White advised the accused of his rights. As other American combat units arrived in III Corps, White also served as defense counsel at pretrial investigations involving soldiers from those units where no judge advocates were available.

McRorie and White also did the full range of legal assistance and handled both military personnel claims and foreign claims. They also made solatium payments. Additionally, both lawyers participated in civil affairs activities, handing out wheat and clothing to the Vietnamese. Capt. White also volunteered to work as an operations officer, pulling a regular shift in the brigade operations shop. Additionally, Gen. Williamson's unhappiness with awards processing in his brigade caused him to shift this duty from the brigade adjutant to McRorie and White. White interviewed soldiers and assembled the award packet resulting in the award of the Medal of Honor to Sgt. Larry S. Pierce, who sacrificed his life when he threw himself onto an exploding antipersonnel mine, saving the lives of his men.[63]

After the departure of McRorie and White, judge advocates continued serving at the 173d, including Capt. Raymond Cole (1966-1967), Maj. Louis F. Musil and Capts. Robert A. Demetz and John D. O'Brien (1967-1968), and Maj. Paul H. Ray and Capts. Peter M. Davenport and L. Dee Oliphant (1968-1969). Like most units, the 173d used nonlawyer officers in courts-martial, even after the effective date of the Military Justice Act of 1968. Thus, Capt. Raymond T. Ruppert, a military intelligence officer who would only later serve in the Judge Advocate General's Corps, was a prosecutor in special courts-martial in September 1969. His defense counsel opponent was a judge advocate.[64]

II Field Force

The II Field Force, a corps-level headquarters formed in Vietnam in March 1966, had operational control of several divisions and numerous nondivisional units. Its area of operations included Saigon and therefore the most heavily populated areas of Vietnam. Lawyering at II Field Force was no different from that done at other combat units in that the assigned judge advocates provided a full range of legal services to both the command group and the soldiers. Judge advocate operations in March 1968 provide a good illustration of how lawyering was done at II Field Force-at least prior to the passage of the Military Justice Act. Although authorized six lawyers, II Field Force had only four: Lt. Col. Irvin M. Kent, Maj. Jon N. Kulish, and Capts. Ned E. Felder and Herbert Green. Kent, who had service as an infantry officer in World War II and later was a civilian attorney on the prosecution staff at the Nuremberg War Crimes Trials, served as

Col. Irvin M. Kent, II Field Force staff judge advocate, 1968-1969. Having twice been wounded while fighting as a platoon leader and rifle company commander in France in World War II, Kent understood the challenges faced by combat commanders in Vietnam—and used his legal skills to enhance mission success.

staff judge advocate. Kulish, a former armor and ordnance officer, was the deputy staff judge advocate as well as the chief of international affairs and legal adviser to units located around the headquarters at Long Binh. Felder, a former Finance Corps officer who had arrived in Vietnam in 1966 with the lead elements of the 4th Infantry Division, was trial counsel for general courts and the claims officer. Green, who had entered the Army directly from civilian life, was the defense counsel and legal assistance officer.

The staff judge advocate, deputy staff judge advocate, and the other lawyers regularly traveled by helicopter to outlying bases of II Field Force. Such trips had many purposes. On 18 March 1968, for example, Lt. Col. Kent traveled to a base camp to investigate a soldier's complaint that his right to speedy trial had been violated by undue delay in the disposition of criminal charges against him. After discussing the issue with the unit commander, Kent also reminded him that claims for damage to personal property caused by hostile action were payable and left forms for the filing of such claims for distribution to unit personnel. When finished with his command advice, Kent set up shop with his

"portable office," an old, battered briefcase containing interview cards, forms for wills and powers of attorney, income tax forms, and absentee voter materials. Kent and the other lawyers always took the legal assistance kit with them on any journey, as every trip away from headquarters was also a legal assistance trip. On this particular visit, Kent assisted five soldiers with federal income tax questions about combat pay exclusion, did two powers of attorney in connection with settling an insurance claim and a real estate transaction, and advised two soldiers on how to contact a stateside lawyer for assistance in divorce proceedings. When he returned to II Field Force headquarters that afternoon, Kent advised on a prisoner of war question. A wounded Vietnamese, present for treatment at a U.S. medical facility, had no identification. He denied being a Viet Cong but admitted that he was avoiding the Vietnamese armed forces draft. As there was no evidence he had committed a hostile act, Kent examined the Geneva Prisoner of War Convention in order to determine whether the man should be released as an innocent civilian, turned over to Vietnamese armed forces law enforcement personnel as a criminal accused, or declared a prisoner of war. Based on the evidence, Kent determined the wounded Vietnamese should be turned over to the police.[65]

On that same day, 18 March 1968, Capt. Green advised a soldier facing trial by summary court-martial of his right to refuse such trial and, if he decided to accept the court-martial, how best to defend himself against the charges. Green also advised the summary court officer on the appropriate procedure and the rights of the accused at a summary court. In addition, Green responded to the staff judge advocate's posttrial review of a general court-martial concluded two weeks previously, advising that additional information about the accused's military record should go to the convening authority prior to his action on the findings and sentence. In addition to this criminal work, Green handled a number of legal assistance clients. One soldier had been named as a party in a civil suit, and Green had moved for a stay of proceedings against the soldier, citing the protections of the Soldiers' and Sailors' Civil Relief Act. That law permitted a soldier absent from a jurisdiction because of military orders to obtain a reasonable delay in civil proceedings until such time as his or her military service either ended or he or she was able to appear in court. Based on Green's motion for a stay, the lawyer representing the plaintiff in the suit agreed to drop the soldier as a party to the action.

Also on that same day, 18 March 1968, Capt. Felder had been awakened at 0200 by the military police. They had a suspect in an aggravated assault case who, after being advised of his rights under Article 31 of the Uniform Code, requested a lawyer prior to questioning. Felder talked privately with the suspect and advised him not make a statement and to decline any further interrogation in the absence of an attorney. After working this case for two more hours, Felder went back to bed at 0400. Only a few hours later, he was back in his office working on a revision of the II Field Force Military Justice Circular. Written as guidance for unit commanders and military policemen, this document explained recent rulings of the U.S. Court of Military Appeals

Capt. Ned E. Felder, the only judge advocate to serve two consecutive twelve-month tours in Vietnam, receives the Bronze Star Medal from Brig. Gen. John S. Lekson, Chief of Staff, II Field Force, Vietnam, in February 1968. After Vietnam, Felder served as a judge advocate at VII Corps and the Berlin Brigade in Germany, and as a military judge. He retired in 1988.

affecting military criminal practice. Among other things, Felder explained that restricting an accused to the limits of a military installation required the government to proceed more quickly to trial. He also explained that an accused's acceptance of nonjudicial punishment under Article 15 was not a basis for finding the accused guilty. Rather, the accused had merely chosen the forum, and the commander still needed proof that an offense was committed before imposing punishment. Later that same day, Felder advised two criminal investigation agents in a case in which he had no attorney-client relationship with the suspect.

Maj. Kulish, the deputy staff judge advocate, was just as busy that same day in March 1968. He examined a posttrial review of a general court-martial for aggravated assault. He advised a battery commander on gathering evidence against a soldier who had assaulted another with a deadly weapon. He executed a special power of attorney for a soldier's wife so that she could settle with his automobile insurance company. He advised another commander on drafting special court-martial charges against a soldier for selling cigarettes in violation of the ration control regulations then in effect. And he counseled a nonlawyer prosecutor in a special court-martial on the method of submitting an official document into evidence as an exception to the hearsay rule. Kulish explained the law on the subject and the method for submitting the document into evidence.[66]

101st Airborne Division (Airmobile)

The 1st Brigade, 101st Airborne Division, and its sole judge advocate, Capt. Frank R. Stone, arrived in Vietnam in July 1965. The division's remaining elements deployed in December 1967. Although its Table of Organization and Equipment authorized five judge advocates, the division had seven lawyers by 1968, headed by Lt. Col. Victor A. DeFiori as staff judge advocate and Maj. Steven R. Norman as deputy staff judge advocate. In accordance with doctrine, DeFiori and most of his lawyers were located at the division rear headquarters at Bien Hoa, outside of Saigon. In December 1969, however, the new division staff judge advocate, Lt. Col. George C. Ryker, moved most of his lawyers to the division main headquarters at Camp Eagle in I Corps. Ryker's rationale was that he and his attorneys would provide better legal support at this location since Maj. Gen. Melvin Zais, the division commander, and his principal staff were there. In addition to Ryker, his deputy, and five judge advocates, the division had at least five more lawyers, both enlisted men and officers.[67] The lawyers worked and lived in wooden huts. Ceiling fans provided some relief from the

In 1968, the "Screaming Legal Eagles" at the 101st Airborne Division's Camp Eagle lived and worked in tents. Here, Lt. Col. Victor A. DeFiori, division staff judge advocate, greets Maj. Gen. Kenneth J. Hodson, The Judge Advocate General, during the latter's inspection tour of legal operations in South Vietnam.

100-degree summer days, but during the monsoon season from November to February almost everyone used an electric blanket or sheet to keep both dry and warm.[68]

Military justice in the 101st Airborne was typical for a deployed division, with the majority of the offenses being absence without leave, disobedience of orders, and assaults. These were prosecuted at general, special, or summary courts, depending on the severity of the offense. Marijuana use generally was handled under Article 15 of the Uniform Code. Special courts were usually tried by a panel; a military judge was used only if the case turned on a particular legal issue. Initially at least, confinement of soldiers before and after trial was a significant problem. Camp Eagle was more than 300 miles from Long Binh jail, the confinement facility for all U.S. Army troops in Vietnam, and it took nearly a week to send two guards on a C-130 aircraft to take or bring back a jailed soldier. Consequently, in December 1969 the division began sending its pretrial and posttrial confinees to the Marine Corps brig in Da Nang. Overall, military justice functioned fairly well, although basic reference materials were often lacking. For example, the division had only one copy of the newly published Manual for Courts-Martial. Its owner was the new deputy staff judge advocate, Maj. Thomas R. Cuthbert, who had received it while attending the new special court judge's course prior to coming to Vietnam. Cuthbert guarded the book closely until more arrived three to six months later.[69]

The amendments to the Uniform Code contained in the Military Justice Act of 1968 were effective on 1 September 1969. Some commanders, however, remained opposed to giving up control over special courts-martial, even after lawyers began serving as defense counsel. For example, in convening special courts, the division's aviation group and artillery commanders continued using nonlawyers as prosecutors, believing that a line officer rather than a judge advocate would better represent the command's interest. These commanders accepted that felony-level general courts required judge advocates, but they did not like the intrusion of lawyers into their special courts, which they saw as tools of discipline rather than instruments of justice. In discussing the merits of the new changes to the Uniform Code, Maj. Cuthbert often heard older officers insist that their experiences as lieutenants prosecuting and defending at special courts demonstrated the fairness of the old system. As nonlawyer trial counsel often did not do well against legally trained defense counsel, however, even the most reluctant special court-martial convening authorities eventually accepted the judge advocate presence at special courts. By mid-1970, when USARV regulations required all jurisdictions in Vietnam to attempt to secure a military judge in all special courts-martial, control over special court proceedings passed irrevocably to military lawyers.[70]

Legal assistance for division soldiers was provided primarily by enlisted lawyers. For example, Pfc. Howard R. Andrews, an Alabama lawyer who had been serving in one of the division's field artillery battalions, joined the legal assistance shop at Camp Eagle. While there, Andrews applied for and received a commission in the Judge Advocate General's Corps, and Maj. Gen. John M. Wright, Zais' successor, personally administered his oath of office on the day Andrews was promoted from private first class to captain. After becoming a judge advocate, Capt. Andrews transferred to the 25th Infantry Division. He was killed in a helicopter crash a few months later.[71]

As the number two lawyer in the division, Maj. Cuthbert did "a little bit of everything," but "because he could speak artillery" by virtue of his prior service as a line officer with the 1st Cavalry Division, his major responsibility became reviewing friendly-fire investigations. Although such investigations could have been conducted pursuant to Army regulations, Generals Zais and Wright wanted friendly-fire incidents investigated under paragraph 32b of the 1969 Manual for Courts-Martial. That provision required a commander with immediate jurisdiction over a wrongdoer to "make or cause to be made, a preliminary inquiry into the charges or the suspected offenses." As a result, an experienced major in the division was directed to interview witnesses and collect other evidence essential to determining fault in a particular friendly-fire incident. After the investigation was complete, Cuthbert reviewed it. This meant examining regulations on fire control and applying the principles of causation and negligence. Often the artillery would claim that the infantry was at fault because the latter had given incorrect map coordinates to fire control. The infantry would deny any map-reading error, asserting firing errors. After receiving Cuthbert's review and pursuing further discussion with principal staff officers in the division, usually the adjutant and operations officer, the division commander took appropriate action. If the investigation found misconduct, the individual at fault usually received an Article 15 as punishment. In one instance, a captain whose firebase was being overrun by the enemy intentionally called for artillery fire on his own position. This act saved many lives, and Gen. Wright recognized the captain's gallantry with the Silver Star. Because the man did not follow fire control procedures, however, Wright also gave him an Article 15.[72]

1st Logistical Command

Established in April 1965, the 1st Logistical Command was a separate major command headed by a two-star Army general. It provided logistics support to all U.S. Army forces in Vietnam except aviation, communications, and military police. By early 1968, 1st Logistical Command had over 55,000 soldiers in more than 600 units located in four support command areas. Between 1965 and 1969, more than forty judge advocates worked at the command's headquarters, first at Tan Son Nhut and later at Long Binh, supporting its country-wide mission.

Col. Hubert E. Miller, two-time Olympian and winner of the Distinguished Service Cross at Normandy, was the staff judge advocate for the 1st Logistical Command from June 1966 to July 1967. He and his legal staff of ten military attorneys handled criminal, procurement, real estate, international, and maritime law. They worked six and a half days a week, twelve hours a day and, although the workload was very heavy, "when the day was over life was fairly good." Capt. Burnett H. Radosh, for example, who was the command's chief of military justice during this time, lived in a "very pleasant" hotel in Saigon. When not writing posttrial reviews, Radosh played poker with his fellow judge advocates and traveled throughout the city.[73]

Col. Hubert E. Miller, the only Army lawyer participant in the Olympics (as a member of the four-man bobsled team, 1952) and recipient of the Distinguished Service Cross (as infantry lieutenant in Normandy, 1944), was the staff judge advocate for 1st Logistical Command from 1966 to 1967. At Miller's suggestion, the command prosecuted the first civilian at a court-martial.

Ninety percent of the workload for Col. Miller and his attorneys involved general courts convened at the command's headquarters. The rapid troop buildup at 1st Logistical Command meant an increase in misconduct and more general courts-martial. Few of the courts-martial were for military offenses. Rather, most were for murders, rapes, and robberies. Unfortunately, the rising crime rate meant that only the most serious cases could be prosecuted at general courts. Thus, some cases that ought to have been general courts resulted in Article 15 proceedings, with the additional "punishment" of reassignment to a "line out-

fit." This was the "big threat" to any soldier who misbehaved in Saigon, as most preferred life in the city to combat duty in the field.[74]

Special courts also were convened at headquarters and at the satellite support commands, but military lawyers generally did not participate in this level of court or in summary courts-martial. The only exception was in the area of civilian misconduct, for it was at 1st Logistical Command that the first civilian was prosecuted at a summary court-martial. A civilian merchant seaman named Bruce was caught stealing from a ship in Cam Ranh Bay and, after being apprehended, was confined in a CONEX container; there was no stockade. After instructing those in charge of the prisoner to give him plenty of water, and without asking for approval from the MACV staff judge advocate, but nonetheless informing him of the Bruce case, Col. Miller conferred with Maj. Gen. Charles W. Eifler, commanding general of the 1st Logistical Command. He proposed to Eifler that a summary court be convened against Bruce and further recommended that an Army lawyer be appointed as summary court officer. Anticipating questions about the command's jurisdiction over a civilian, Eifler signed a memorandum prepared by Miller. This document, dated 8 December 1966, stated that "in view of the conditions now prevailing in Vietnam, I have determined that 'time of war' within the meaning of the UCMJ exists in this area of operations."[75] First Logistical Command Special Orders then were published appointing Capt. Radosh as summary court officer. Radosh traveled to Cam Ranh Bay, heard the evidence against Bruce, and convicted him. Bruce's punishment was a reprimand, a fine, and restriction to his ship. Col. Miller reviewed the abbreviated record of the summary court and Gen. Eifler approved the findings and sentence.[76] Although 1st Logistical Command lawyers conducted the proceedings against Bruce, both USARV and MACV headquarters certainly approved of Miller's action, as did civilian officials at the American embassy.[77]

In addition to prosecuting the first civilian in Vietnam, 1st Logistical Command also processed the first enlisted resignation in lieu of court-martial. A sergeant and some other men had stolen a jeep and some radios, dug a hole, and buried them, planning to retrieve the property later. The sergeant was found out, however, and charges were preferred for larceny of government property. Prior to trial, however, Col. Miller suggested to the accused's defense counsel that the soldier "consider a resignation in lieu of trial" under Army Regulation 635-200. This regulation, governing enlisted personnel separations, had a new provision whereby a soldier pending trial for an offense punishable by a punitive discharge could request "a discharge for the good of the service in lieu of trial." The defense counsel had never heard of this new provision, but he advised his client to request the discharge. Miller took the request to Eifler who, though also unfamiliar with the new provision, approved it. The soldier had a good record so he got a break, receiving a general rather than an undesirable discharge. Interestingly, it was Miller who first proposed creating an enlisted resignation in lieu of court-martial when he was working in the Pentagon at the Judge Advocate General's Military Justice Branch from 1960 to 1963. Under then existing law, an officer could resign in lieu of court-martial, but enlisted soldiers had no comparable mechanism. Believing that the enlisted ranks should have the same right as officers, and that authorizing a discharge in lieu of trial would avoid unnecessary criminal work, Col. Miller sent his proposal forward for staffing, but no action was taken. However, during a later visit with then-Brig. Gen. Hodson, the assistant judge advocate general for military justice, Miller again suggested that creating this enlisted resignation mechanism was a good idea. Hodson agreed, picked up the telephone, and spoke personally with the Adjutant General, requesting speedy approval of Miller's proposal. The new provision appeared in the July 1966 revised version of Army Regulation 635-200.[78]

U.S. Army Trial Judiciary, Vietnam

The rapid buildup of American troops meant more courts-martial, particularly general courts. Consequently, a new judicial circuit consisting of two law officers was created in Vietnam in October 1965.[79] The small number of general courts-martial tried in Vietnam in late 1965 and early 1966 meant that a law officer traveled to Vietnam on temporary duty to judge the case. As general courts increased, however, a more permanent presence was needed in Vietnam, and by 1967 there were two law officers assigned for duty in country. Lt. Col. Paul Durbin, who had been the first judge advocate in Vietnam from 1959 to 1961, was one of them. Durbin volunteered to return to Vietnam and was first assigned as staff judge advocate for the newly created II Field Force. After his promotion to colonel, however, Durbin was asked if he would like to be the law officer in Vietnam. When he agreed, he returned to the Judge Advocate General's School in Charlottesville, Virginia, for a short course on military judging. He then returned to be the only military judge in Vietnam until the arrival of Col. James C. Waller. Durbin and Waller tried cases seven days a week. Sometimes they used a chapel as their courtroom.[80]

Durbin's most memorable case involved the rape and murder of a twenty-year-old Vietnamese woman named Phan Thi Mao. On 17 November 1966, Sgt. David E. Gervase and Pfc. Steven C. Thomas, both members of C Company, 2d Battalion (Airborne), 8th Cavalry, 1st Cavalry Division, talked with three other squad members about plans to kidnap a "pretty girl" during a reconnaissance mission planned for the next day. Gervase talked about having sex with the woman and then killing her.

Early on the morning of 18 November, the squad entered a village of about a half-dozen huts looking for a woman. After finding Phan Thi Mao, they bound her wrists with a rope, gagged her, and took her on the mission. Then, after setting up headquarters in an abandoned hut, four of the soldiers raped her. The next day, in the midst of a firefight with the Viet Cong, Thomas and Gervase became worried that the woman would be seen with the squad. Thomas then took the woman into a brushy area and stabbed her three times with a hunting knife. The woman, however, did not die. When she tried to flee, three of the soldiers chased her. Thomas caught her and shot her in the head with his M16 rifle. The real hero of the case was Pfc. Robert M. Storeby, who reported the crime. At first, the chain of command, including the company commander, took no action. Storeby, despite threats against his life by the soldiers who raped and murdered the woman, was determined to see the soldiers punished. His persistence in reporting the crime to higher authorities eventually resulted in general courts-martial against Gervase and Thomas, as well as against Pfc. Cipriano S. Garcia and Pfc. Joseph C. Garcia. All four men were convicted of rape and murder in March and April 1967. At the trial of Thomas, who had done the actual stabbing and shooting, the prosecutor asked the jury to impose a death sentence. The court, however, instead sentenced Thomas to life imprisonment. Joseph Garcia received 15 years in jail, Gervase 10 years in jail, and Cipriano Garcia 4 years' confinement. All four were dishonorably discharged from the Army. Some twenty years later, these courts-martial became the basis for the Columbia Pictures motion picture "Casualties of War."[81]

Until the passage of the Military Justice Act of 1968, there was, of course, no lawyer involvement at special courts-martial. Nonlawyer line officers, usually lieutenants, served as trial and defense counsel. There was no military judge or law officer either; the senior officer on the panel presided over the special court. The new legislation, however, meant that after 1 September 1969 judge advocates would be needed as special court military judges. In Vietnam, the Judge Advocate

General's Corps took a two-pronged approach in satisfying this new need: two Army lawyers would be full-time special court judges and a number of other judge advocates would serve as part-time military judges.

The first two full-time special court-martial judges in Vietnam were Maj. John F. Naughton and Maj. Dennis R. Hunt. Hunt, a graduate of Harvard Law School, entered the Judge Advocate General's Corps in January 1965. After a tour with the 2d Infantry Division in Korea and at the Appellate Division at the Judge Advocate General's Office in Washington, Maj. Hunt volunteered for duty in Vietnam in August 1969.[82]

Assigned to Long Binh in the 17th Army Judicial Circuit, Hunt traveled six days a week for a year, sitting as a judge in 320 courts-martial. The most common offenses were absence without leave, violating lawful general regulations, and possession and use of marijuana or barbiturates, but Maj. Hunt also presided over eleven homicide prosecutions. More than 90 percent of the defendants opted for trial by military judge alone. One result of choosing a bench trial was that "legal niceties" were more important than in a trial by members in which the senior officer controlled the proceedings. Thus, Hunt ruled on evidentiary issues such as whether a commander's search and seizure of an accused's living area was based on probable cause and whether two military policemen who stopped a soldier for being in an off-limits area exceeded the scope of a "pat down" search for weapons in looking in the accused's sock. Judge Hunt determined that they had.[83]

One interesting aspect of trial by special courts-martial during Hunt's tenure was that a unit's manpower concerns often outweighed the need for punishment. Court members sentencing an accused might adjudge confinement as a part of a sentence, but the convening authority often suspended any sentence to imprisonment, recognizing that, for some soldiers, a stockade might seem preferable to combat. Later, this practice of suspending a sentence to confinement was institutionalized. USARV Supplement 1 to Army Regulation 27-10 required any sentence to confinement be suspended unless a punitive discharge also was adjudged, the accused had a prior conviction, or it was an "exceptional case involving serious offenses."[84]

Summing Up

The more than 350 judge advocates who lawyered in Vietnam from 1965 to 1969 were challenged as never before. The MACV advisory and USARV claims programs showed how law might be used to further not only the command's mission, but also the American policy of strengthening the democratic process in Vietnam. USARV judge advocates and Army attorneys at the field forces, divisions, and other combat and support units were prosecuting and defending courts-martial in a combat environment, and doing so while implementing important changes in military criminal law. No matter how much Army lawyers supported the command and its mission, however, legal services for soldiers remained a priority as well.

Just as in the early years of the Vietnam conflict, a significant number of judge advocates serving in Vietnam between 1965 and 1969 also enhanced mission success in ways not normally done by judge advocates. Capt. Sherwood, while a member of the MACV SJA Advisory Division, illustrated how being an excellent soldier made a judge advocate even more valuable in the field. Col. Haughney, in

July 1968: Lt. Col. Hugh J. Clausen, Staff Judge Advocate, 1st Infantry Division (left), and Lt. Col. Thomas C. Oldham, Deputy Staff Judge Advocate, U.S. Army, Vietnam, stand at the entrance to the staff judge advocate's bunker at Lai Khe. Clausen was the Judge Advocate General from 1981 to 1985.

taking the initiative to resolve several prisoner of war issues, proved that Army lawyers can-and should-handle such nonlegal matters if necessary. Col. Williams, in providing legal advice to the U.S. ambassador and in participating as a member of the Irregular Practices Committee, illustrated how Army lawyers must be prepared to work closely with high-level, nonmilitary government officials. And Col. Miller, in arranging for the court-martial of a civilian merchant sailor, proved that Army lawyers and military law could be used to promote good order and discipline among all American citizens accompanying the U.S. armed forces in Vietnam.

Moreover, events in Vietnam set in motion the forces that would result in an institutional change in the role played by Army lawyers. The uproar over the 1968 killings at My Lai, the findings contained in the 1970 Peers Report, and Col. Solf's 1972 proposal for a Department of Defense Law of War program all resulted in a new responsibility for Army judge advocates in 1974: to ensure that all future U.S. military operations strictly complied with the Law of War.

As the U.S. troop buildup reached its peak, judge advocate operations in Vietnam also reached their zenith-at least in terms of the number of Army lawyers deployed to that part of the world and the huge volume of work done by them. After 1969, the work done by judge advocates was certainly similar to that conducted by their colleagues between 1966 and 1969. Yet there also were some new challenges. More than anything, Army lawyers in Vietnam from 1970 to 1975 wrestled with legal issues accompanying the U.S. troop withdrawal from Vietnam.

Notes

1. Interv, author with Prugh, 25 Sep 96.

2. Demma, "U.S. Army in Vietnam," 638-39.

3. George S. Eckhardt, *Command and Control: 1950-1969, Vietnam Studies* (Washington, D.C.: Government Printing Office, 1974), 54.

4. Demma, "U.S. Army in Vietnam," 642.

5. Prugh, *Law at War*, 88.

6. Clarke, *The Final Years*, 93.

7. Demma, "U.S. Army in Vietnam," 649. For a perspective on small-unit operations in Vietnam, see James McDonough, *Platoon Leader* (Novato, Calif.: Presidio Press, 1985), and David Donovan, *Once a Warrior King* (New York: McGraw-Hill, 1985). McDonough served as an infantry lieutenant with the 173d Airborne Brigade in 1970; Donovan served with a province advisory team in the Mekong Delta in 1969.

8. Prugh, *Law at War*, 100.

9. Ibid., 10, 12.

10. Ibid., 53.

11. Interv, author with Col Edward W. Haughney, 27 Sep 96, Historians files, OTJAG.

12. MACV Directive 20-5, Prisoners of War-Determination of Eligibility, 21 Sep 66, Historians files, OTJAG.

13. Prugh, *Law at War*, 65-66.

14. Guenter Lewy, *America in Vietnam* (New York: Oxford University Press, 1978), 364; interv, author with Prugh, 25 Sep 96; Prugh, *Law at War*, app. F.

15. Prugh, *Law at War*, 74; Lewy, *America in Vietnam*, 325, 348; Rpt, Clerk of Court, U.S. Army Judiciary, Convictions by General and Special (BCD) Courts-Martial of Offenses Against Vietnamese, 1965-1973, n.d., Historians files, OTJAG; United States v. McGee, CM 422412 (1969), (court admonished soldier after convicting him of involuntary manslaughter); United States v. Hodges, CM 420341 (1969), (sergeant cut off heads of dead enemy soldiers and posed for photographs with the corpses). See also United States v. Lund, United States v. Francis, CM 420181 (1969), (rape of Vietnamese female by two Americal Division soldiers); United States v. Woods, CM 416803 (1966), (soldier killed detainee allegedly on instructions of company commander); United States v. Williams, CM 419872 (1968), (soldier convicted of conduct prejudicial to good order and discipline for cutting off ears and index fingers of

Vietnamese corpse); United States v. Goldman, CM 420332, 43 CMR 77, ACMR (1970), (company commander convicted for failing to report noncombat death of detainee and dereliction of duty in failing to protect Vietnamese female in custody of his unit); United States v. Duffy, CM 424795, 47 CMR 658 (ACMR 1973), (lieutenant convicted of involuntary manslaughter for causing Vietnamese to be taken to a woodline and shot with a rifle). For a more thorough discussion of American war crimes in Vietnam, see Lewy, *America in Vietnam*, 323-441.

16. Prugh, *Law at War*, 90.

17. Ibid., 91; MACV Directive 27-6, par. 2(b)(2), reprinted in Prugh, *Law at War*, app. J.

18. Prugh, *Law at War*, 108-09.

19. Trip Report on Vietnam, Eugene T. Herbert, Department of State, 30 Dec 66, sub: Status of Civilian Contractors in Vietnam, box 1, HQ, MACV Staff Judge Advocate, General Records, RG 472, NARA.

20. Memo, Staff Judge Advocate, 1st Logistical Command, for Commanding General, USA Support Command, 13 Mar 67, sub: Court-martial jurisdiction over civilians, box 1, USARV Staff Judge Advocate Section, Administrative Office, RG 472, NARA.

21. Interv, author with Haughney, 27 Sep 96; Gary D. Solis, *Marines and Military Law in Vietnam: Trial by Fire* (Washington, D.C.: Government Printing Office, 1989), 99-100.

22. Prugh, *Law at War*, 93.

23. Ibid., 104.

24. "Scrips to replace the U.S. dollars today," Saigon Post, 31 Aug 65. For additional details on the Military Payment Certificate program, see Prugh, *Law at War*, 104-06.

25. "Minutes, U.S. Irregular Practices Committee," 3 Jun 70, Folder 401-05, Irregular Practices Committee, 1970, box 1, HQ, MACV Staff Judge Advocate, General Records, RG 472, NARA.

26. Staff Study, The Role of Civil Law in Counterinsurgency, HQ, MACV, May 65, Historians files, OTJAG.

27. MACV Directive 25-1, Claims, 14 May 65, Historians files, OTJAG.

28. Interv, author with Prugh, 25 Sep 96; Prugh, *Law at War*, 83; U.S. Public Law 90-521, sec. 3 (1968), amending Title 10, United States Code, sec. 2734.

29. Prugh, *Law at War*, 41, 49.

30. Staff Study, Transfer of MACV Staff Elements to USARV, HQ MACV, 28 Nov 65, box 1, USARV Staff Judge Advocate Section, Administrative Office, RG 472, NARA.

31. Ltr, Prugh to Adelaide Hunt, 22 Mar 65, Historians files, OTJAG.

32. Prugh Jnl, 23 Apr 65, Historians files, OTJAG; Prugh, *Law at War*, 47-48, 53, 115.

33. Prugh, *Law at War*, 50.

34. Ibid.

35. Ibid., 54-55.

36. Memo, USARV Staff Judge Advocate for USARV Assistant Chief of Staff, Comptroller, 12 Sep 68, sub: Mission of USARV SJA, box 1, USARV Staff Judge Advocate Section, Administrative Office, RG 472, NARA.

37. Interv, author with Col John Jay Douglass, 19 Nov 96, Historians files, OTJAG.

38. Uniform Code of Military Justice, art. 36, Title 10, United States Code, sec. 836; *The Army Lawyer: A History of the Judge Advocate General's Corps, 1775-1975* (Washington, D.C.: Government Printing Office, 1975), 244-45.

39. For a detailed analysis of the Military Justice Act of 1968, see Samuel J. Ervin, "The Military Justice Act of 1968," Wake Forest Law Review 5 (1969):223; Kenneth J. Hodson, "The Military Justice Act," Judge Advocate Journal, Bull number 42 (May 1970):30.

40. *Army Lawyer*, 247.

41. Ibid.

42. Interv, author with Maj Gen William K. Suter, 25 Jul 96, Historians files, OTJAG.

43. Interv, Maj Dan Wright and Capt James Rupper with Maj Gen Wilton B. Persons, Jr., 16 Jan 85, p. 14, Historians files, OTJAG.

44. Interv, author with Maj Gen Wilton B. Persons, Jr., 17 Sep 96, Historians files, OTJAG.

45. Dennis R. Hunt, "Viet Nam Hustings," Judge Advocate Journal, Bull no. 44 (July 1972):23.

46. William H. Hammond, *Public Affairs: The Military and the Media, 1968-1973, The U.S. Army in Vietnam* (Washington, D.C.: Government Printing Office, 1996), 220-24.

47. Michael Bilton and Kevin Sim, *Four Hours in My Lai* (New York: Viking Press, 1992), 329.

48. Hammond, *Military and the Media, 1968-1973*, 252.

49. Ibid., 258-59; Lewy, *America in Vietnam*, 356-58; United States v. Calley, 46 CMR 1131 (ACMR 1973); interv, author with Col William G. Eckhardt, 8 Dec 98, Historians files, OTJAG. See also Calley v. Callaway, 382 Federal Supplement (F. Suppl.) 650 (1974).

50. Report of the Department of the Army Review of the Preliminary Investigations into the My Lai Incident (Peers Inquiry), 14 Mar 70, I:10-26; Hammond, *Military and the Media, 1968-1973*, 244-45; Army Regulation (AR) 35-216, Training: The Geneva Conventions of 1949 and Hague Convention No. IV of 1907, 28 May 1970; DOD Directive 5100.77, DOD Program for Implementation of the Law of War, 5 Nov 74.

51. Hammond, *Military and the Media, 1968-1973*, 139.

52. Interv, author with Brig Gen Bruce C. Babbitt, 16 Sep 96, Historians files, OTJAG.

53. J. Stevens Berry, *Those Gallant Men* (Novato, Calif.: Presidio Press, 1984), 51-52; interv, author with Berry, 10 Jul 96, Historians files, OTJAG. For a detailed examination of the Green Beret murder case, see Jeff Stein, *A Murder in Wartime* (New York: St. Martin's Press, 1992).

54. Hammond, *Military and the Media, 1968-1973*, 144. See also Wright and Rupper, interv with Persons, 16 Jan 85, 44-88.

55. Ltr, OTJAG, DA, to SJA, USARV, 27 Feb 69, sub: United Fruit Co. v. US, box 2, USARV Staff Judge Advocate Section, Litigation Case Files, RG 472, NARA.

56. Ltr, OTJAG, DA, to SJA, USARV, 28 Oct 69, sub: Donald W. Morrison v. US, box 2, USARV Staff Judge Advocate Section, Litigation Case Files, RG 472, NARA. See also Morrison v. United States, F. Supp. 316 (1970):78.

57. George S. Prugh, "Law Practice in the Vietnam War," Federal Bar Journal 27 (1967):58.

58. Prugh, *Law at War*, 83.

59. Ibid., 62.

60. Interv, author with Lt Col Leonard G. Crowley, 24 Jul 96, Historians files, OTJAG.

61. Ibid.; Hammond, *Military and the Media, 1968-1973*, 144.

62. Interv, author with Holdaway, 24 Jul 96.

63. Interv, author with Col Charles A. White, Jr., 20 Sep 96, Historians files, OTJAG.

64. Interv, author with Col Raymond T. Ruppert, 2 Oct 96, Historians files, OTJAG.

65. Irvin M. Kent, Jon N. Kulish, Ned E. Felder, and Herbert Green, "A Lawyer's Day in Vietnam," American Bar Association Journal 54 (December 1968):1177-78; Pierre Loomis, "Circuit Riding Judge," Hurricane (July 1968):6.

66. Kent, et al., "A Lawyer's Day in Vietnam," 1179-82.

67. Judge Advocate General's Corps, U.S. Army, Personnel Directory, 1967, 1968, Historians files, OTJAG.

68. Interv, author with Brig Gen Thomas R. Cuthbert, 2 Oct 96, Historians files, OTJAG.

69. Ibid.

70. Ibid.; USARV Supp. 1 to AR 27-10, Military Justice, par. 2-15b, 15 Jun 70.

71. Interv, author with Cuthbert, 2 Oct 96; interv, author with Col Burnett H. Radosh, 10 Jul 96, Historians files, OTJAG.

72. Interv, author with Cuthbert, 2 Oct 96.

73. Interv, author with Radosh, 10 Jul 96.

74. Interv, author with Col Hubert E. Miller, 2 Jul 96, Historians files, OTJAG.

75. Memo, CG, 1st Logistical Command, for CG, USA Support Command, Cam Ranh Bay, 8 Dec 66, sub: Jurisdiction over Civilians, Historians files, OTJAG.

76. Interv, author with Miller, 2 Jul 96.

77. Trip Report on Vietnam, Eugene T. Herbert, Department of State, 30 Dec 66, sub: Status of Civilian Contractors in Viet Nam, box 1, MACV Staff Judge Advocate, General Records, RG 472, NARA.

78. AR 635-200, Personnel Separations, Enlisted Personnel, 15 Jul 66; interv, author with Miller, 10 Oct 96.

79. *Army Lawyer*, 240.

80. Interv, author with Durbin, 1 Jul 96.

81. United States v. Steven C. Thomas, CM 416162, 38 CMR 655 (ABMR 1968); United States v. David E. Gervase, CM 416161, 22 Mar 67; United States v. Joseph C. Garcia, CM 416160, 17 Mar 67; United States v. Cipriano S. Garcia, CM 416159, 38 CMR 625 (ABMR 1967); interv, author with Durbin, 11 Jul 96; interv, author with Eckhardt, 8 Dec 98; see also Daniel Lang, *Casualties of War* (New York: McGraw, 1969).

82. Interv, author with Col Dennis R. Hunt, 13 Sep 96, Historians files, OTJAG.

83. Hunt, "Viet Nam Hustings," 15, 26; interv, author with Hunt, 13 Sep 96.

84. USARV Supplement 1 to AR 27-10, par. 2-35, 15 Jun 70; interv, author with Hunt, 13 Sep 96. For another firsthand account of judging in Vietnam, see Jack H. Crouchet, *Vietnam Stories: A Judge's Memoir* (Niwot, Colo.: University Press of Colorado, 1997).

Chapter 3

Vietnam: Lawyering in the Final Years 1970-1975

"Prior to going to Vietnam, I was the Staff Judge Advocate at the 3d Infantry Division and V Corps . . . those were normal assignments . . . Vietnam was chaos."[1]

—Brig. Gen. Joseph N. Tenhet, Jr., Staff Judge Advocate, U.S. Army, Vietnam, and Military Assistance Command, Vietnam (1972-1973)

Background

Although American offensive operations continued after 1970, President Richard M. Nixon had decided the year before to withdraw U.S. forces from Vietnam. He called his strategy "Vietnamization," and its intent was to create a strong South Vietnamese military capable of carrying the main burden of fighting so that the Americans could depart. Under the new strategy, all American operations aimed to buy time for the South Vietnamese, whose improvement and modernization promised to be hard going whatever the good intentions all around. Chief targets for U.S. forces were enemy bases in South Vietnam and over the borders. Their denial as staging areas for enemy operations seemed the surest way of reducing the long-term threat to South Vietnam.

As a result, while American troops began withdrawing, with most units leaving in 1970 and 1971, aggressive operations continued, some of them very large scale. One of the largest kicked off on 1 May 1970, as units of the 1st Cavalry Division, 25th Infantry Division, and 11th Armored Cavalry Regiment pushed into Cambodia. The Americans discovered large, well-stocked storage sites, training camps, and hospitals, all recently occupied. But most enemy units retreated deep into the country, beyond the self-imposed limit of the U.S. advance. Despite mixed success in Cambodia, the Vietnamese, with U.S. aviation support, launched across the border into Laos in February 1971. The aim was to sever the Ho Chi Minh Trail, the enemy supply line into South Vietnam. The result, however, was near-disaster for the South Vietnamese, whose operational weakness at all levels of their army was painfully and embarrassingly revealed.[2]

The continued withdrawal of U.S. forces meant decreasing mobility, firepower, intelligence support, and air support. In 1970 there were 5,000 American helicopters in Vietnam; by 1972, there were about 500. When the North Vietnamese Army launched its Easter offensive in March 1972, total U.S. military strength in theater was about 95,000, of which 6,000 were combat troops. In these circumstances, responsibility for countering the enemy invasion fell almost completely on the South Vietnamese Army, by now a well-armed fighting force. Its poorly skilled soldiers and leaders, however, were no match for the North Vietnamese, who defeated the South Vietnamese 3d Infantry Division and seized most of the northernmost province before U.S. air power blunted the assault.[3]

The United States, North and South Vietnam, and the Viet Cong signed in January 1973 an armistice that promised a cease-fire and national reconciliation. Immediately, U.S. Army, Vietnam, and Military Assistance Command, Vietnam, were dissolved, all remaining U.S. troops were pulled out, and American military action in Vietnam halted. U.S. advisers, who until the end had provided backbone for the South Vietnamese command structure, were also withdrawn.[4]

But far from ending the fighting, the signing of the armistice and the departure of the Americans left South Vietnamese forces competing with the enemy for territory. Unfortunately, the combat capability of the South Vietnamese military was now on a downward slope, in part because poor maintenance and lack of spare parts made essential equipment inoperable. When a weary Congress reduced U.S. military aid, Saigon had no choice but to avoid engaging in combat operations to husband its diminishing resources. The end was not long in coming. In January 1975 the North Vietnamese seized Phuoc Long Province in III Corps and, when the United States did not respond, continued the offensive. When President Nguyen Van Thieu withdrew his forces to defend Saigon to the south, this action, though sound, provoked panic among both troops and civilians. Some South Vietnamese units fought well, but most disintegrated. Saigon fell to the enemy on 30 April 1975, and American technicians, embassy personnel, and others were evacuated that day.[5]

Lawyering at Military Assistance Command, Vietnam

From 1970 to 1973 the number of Army lawyers at MACV headquarters ranged from three to five, with an Army colonel continuing as the staff judge advocate. Col. Robert K. Weaver held the position from July 1970 to June 1971. His successor, Col. Lawrence P. Hansen, remained in Saigon for only three months, from June to August 1971, before Col. James F. Senechal replaced him in November 1971. Senechal was destined to be the last MACV staff judge advocate; when American facilities closed at Long Binh in December 1972, Col. Joseph N. Tenhet, Jr., the USARV staff judge advocate, was selected to stay in Vietnam as the new USARV/MACV staff judge advocate. Senechal departed for the United States.

MACV Advisory Division

MACV judge advocates provided the same kind of legal services as their predecessors, but what differentiated their lawyering in Vietnam from the practice of others was their advisory work with the Vietnamese. In Saigon, these efforts focused on the organization and budget of the Directorate of Military Justice. The Americans also collected, translated, and indexed Vietnamese laws and decrees, prepared staff studies, and participated as members of various MACV and joint MACV-Vietnamese committees. For example, a MACV judge advocate adviser was a member of the joint committee developing a national mobilization study for the Vietnamese armed forces in the fall of 1972. MACV lawyers also continued to participate in the Law Society of Free Vietnam and Law Day activities.

Also as before, the MACV Advisory Division taught courses in government and law at the University of Saigon and taught English to Vietnamese lawyers who were then, or later became, Supreme Court justices, ministers of justice and interior, or key Directorate of Military Justice personnel. This Saigon-based educational program lasted until USARV/MACV judge advocate operations ceased in March 1973. Complementing MACV advisory work was a program for study in the United States. MACV lawyers arranged for selected Vietnamese lawyers to visit the United States under the auspices of the State Department's Foreign Leader and Specialist Program. They also selected Vietnamese judge advocates for military law instruction at the Judge Advocate General's School in Charlottesville, Virginia. An average of two Vietnamese officers a year were sent to Charlottesville, with a high point reached in January 1970 when four officers qualified for attendance at the school's eight-week basic course or the nine-month advanced course. The Americans believed that emphasizing and encouraging education promoted respect for the law and prompted the Vietnamese to take fresh approaches to legal education. In November 1971, when the Directorate of Military Justice opened its own school for training military lawyers, administrative personnel, and court clerks, it came as no surprise to American advisers that the school's new staff included two Vietnamese judge advocates who had studied in the United States thanks to a MACV Advisory Division initiative.[6]

Outside Saigon, field advisory activities varied widely. Some judge advocates worked with their Vietnamese counterparts on a daily basis and devoted most of their time to Vietnamese military justice procedures, the operation of Vietnamese provincial jails and military prisons, the Vietnamese claims program, desertion control, resources control, and security programs. As the judge advocate field advisers were collocated with the senior U.S. adviser, they sometimes functioned as command judge advocates. What a field adviser did, and the success of his tour of duty, depended on many factors: his own personality, his ability to establish rapport with his Vietnamese colleague, the level of support given to him by the local U.S. commander, and the legal needs of the time and place. More than anything else, however, a field adviser had to be innovative, identifying problems and discovering practical solutions. Sometimes the most pressing problems were nonlegal, such as arranging transportation for Vietnamese legal officers, providing storage for records of trial, or obtaining materials and equipment to improve the Vietnamese military courts and prisons.[7]

Although most advisory efforts continued programs in existence, one new challenge was working with the Vietnamese military prison system. In the American Army, confinement facilities are the responsibility of the Military Police Corps. In the Vietnamese armed forces, prisons were administered by the Military Justice Corps. Consequently, as judge advocates were advisers to the Directorate of Military Justice, they also became advisers to the military prisons. This was a role for which Army lawyers had little preparation.

Advisory efforts at the military prisons fell into two categories: providing administrative guidance and technical expertise, and obtaining building materials and supplies. Officers from the MACV staff judge advocate's office in Saigon periodically visited the military prison in each corps area, monitoring progress and coordinating advisory programs with the field advisers. Recognizing that the Vietnamese badly needed professional help with their prison system and that his lawyers lacked expertise, Col. Weaver, the MACV staff judge advocate from July 1970 to June 1971, augmented the Advisory Division staff with a U.S. Military Police Corps officer. This man, whom Weaver assigned as a special adviser to the pretrial confinement facilities under Vietnamese control, prepared an administrative checklist for those facilities. This was translated into Vietnamese and presented to the Directorate of Military Justice as a vehicle for improving conditions and a model for any future procedural innovations.[8]

Judge Advocate Operations at U.S. Army, Vietnam

Until December 1972, when U.S. Army, Vietnam, merged with the Military Assistance Command, USARV judge advocates provided the same range of legal services-military justice, administrative law, legal assistance, and claims-offered by their predecessors. The number of military lawyers at USARV headquarters from 1970 to 1972 ranged from eight to twelve. Judge advocates of note included Col. Wilton B. Persons, Jr., later the judge advocate general; Maj. William K. Suter, later the assistant judge advocate general; and Lt. Col. Lloyd K. Rector, a future brigadier general in the Judge Advocate General's Corps. The changing membership of the corps was reflected in the assignment of a husband-and-wife "JAG team" to Vietnam, with Capt. Nancy W. Keough at U.S. Army Area Command and Capt. James E. Keough at U.S. Army Procurement Agency. Although not the first, Nancy Keough was one of the few female judge advocates to serve in Vietnam.[9]

Military Justice

After 1970, USARV lawyers handled all courts-martial in The Support Troops, Vietnam. With more than 40,000 personnel, it was the largest general court-martial jurisdiction in Vietnam. These same attorneys also provided guidance and assistance to thirteen subordinate general courts-martial jurisdictions and about a hundred special court-martial convening authorities. The many special court jurisdictions resulted from Article 23 of the Uniform Code. That

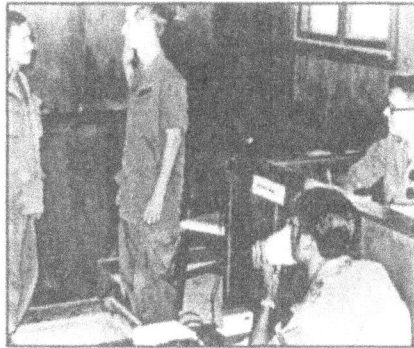

After the passage of the Military Justice Act of 1968, Army lawyers began participating in courts-martial as military judges. In this photograph, circa 1970, a judge advocate captain presides as a military judge at a special court-martial. Except for the jungle fatigues, court proceedings in Vietnam were no different than those held in the United States and Europe.

provision permitted the commanding officer of a detached battalion to convene a special court. In Vietnam, this meant that some divisions had as many as fifteen special court-martial convening authorities. With the passage of the Military Justice Act of 1968 and the resulting lawyer participation at special courts-martial, so many convening authorities made managing legal activity more difficult. Lawyers, court reporters, and legal clerks who previously had limited roles in the operation of special courts now discovered that prosecuting, defending, transcribing, and processing these courts-martial had increased their work more than twentyfold in just a year, and that the existence of so many convening authorities only added to the chaos.[10] Consequently, Col. Persons, as USARV staff judge advocate, urged field force and division staff judge advocates to convince their commanding generals to consolidate their special courts at the brigade level. Most did, but some did not. Uniformity in military justice matters therefore remained problematic.[11]

Was military justice working at U.S. Army, Vietnam, and at the corps, division, and brigade levels? Did the system serve both justice and discipline? The answer depended on who was asked, at what level that person worked in the system, and the time period in reference. From 1965 on, almost all Army lawyers working at the trial level-staff judge advocates, trial and defense counsel, and judges-believed that the criminal law system worked well in Vietnam. They observed that commanders routinely used courts-martial to punish any serious disobedience of lawful authority. Murder, rape, robbery, and other criminal offenses were successfully prosecuted. These prosecutions, and the use of nonjudicial proceedings under Article 15, promoted good order and discipline. But justice was also done and, rather than harming the system as some had feared, the Military Justice Act of 1968 bettered it. On 10 August 1970, Brig. Gen. Harold E. Parker, assistant judge advocate general of the Army, reported that after a full year's experience under the new act, the "military justice system had substantially improved in regards both efficiency and fairness." Legally qualified counsel were representing the accused at special courts and military judges were being detailed in about 85 percent of such courts, and this number was expected to increase. Additionally, prior to the act, all trials were by jury. Afterward, accused were selecting trial by judge alone 85 percent of the time at general courts and 95 percent of the time at special courts. Since the Army tried 300 general courts and 4,964 special courts in Vietnam in 1970, this "brought about a decrease in trial time, shortened trial records, and has resulted in a significant saving of line officer time."[12] While there is no doubt that the trial-by-judge procedure streamlined criminal justice, the system's main strength was the cadre of judge advocates who were committed to making it work. They journeyed by airplane, helicopter, truck, and jeep throughout the theater, prosecuting, defending, and judging courts-martial, often at considerable risk. More than a few records of trial note: "The personnel of the court, counsel, and the accused recessed to nearby bunkers because of a VC rocket and mortar attack."[13] In the end, courts-martial that needed trying were tried.

At the same time, while thousands of courts-martial were successfully prosecuted in Vietnam, a challenge to the military justice system was arising in another quarter. The symptoms were Armywide and its sources were even broader, although on this point there was considerable controversy.[14] But whatever the origins, the breakdown of order and discipline in the Army, beginning in the late 1960s, created extraordinary institutional turbulence in Vietnam and raised questions about the Uniform Code and military justice in general. The Army, like the nation, was knee-deep in a crisis of confidence in its mission as fewer and fewer soldiers, especially young draftees, were satisfied to risk their lives in an unpopular war.

The signs of discontent were everywhere: drug addiction, racial strife, and mutinous behavior on the battlefield. Some 144 underground newspapers published on, or aimed at, U.S. military bases encouraged disobedience and dissent. "In Vietnam," wrote the Fort Lewis-McChord Free Press in Washington, "the Lifers, the Brass, are the true Enemy, not the enemy." Another West Coast newspaper advised its readers: "Don't desert. Go to Vietnam and kill your commanding officer." Demoralized, some soldiers turned to alcohol. Drugs, almost as easily obtained, were also increasingly attractive, leading a congressional investigating subcommittee to report in April 1971 that "10 to 15% of our troops in Vietnam are now using high-grade heroin."[15] A September 1971 study done by the White House showed that almost 69 percent of soldiers leaving Vietnam had experimented with marijuana; 38 percent said they had tried opium and 34 percent heroin.[16] By the end of American involvement in the war, "more soldiers were being evacuated to the United States for drug problems than for wounds."[17]

Army leaders looked to the military justice system as a weapon in the fight against rampant drug use. In 1970, Army authorities in Vietnam arrested 11,058 soldiers for illegal drug possession, sale, or use-of which 1,146 involved either opium or heroin.[18] Many of these resulted in courts-martial. A majority of the general courts prosecuted by Maj.

Francis A. Gilligan at U.S. Army Support Command, Saigon, from July 1970 to July 1971 concerned drugs.[19] Similarly, Capt. James O. Smyser, assigned to the support command from August 1971 to June 1972, quickly discovered that many of the roughly 200 courts-martial he prosecuted or defended were for drugs, usually heroin and other highly addictive substances.[20] And even successful soldiers had drug problems. When Capt. Barry P. Steinberg, serving as a full-time special court judge from June 1971 to February 1972, asked an accused for the story behind the Silver Star ribbon he wore on his uniform, the man told him that he could not remember as he had been "strung out on heroin" at the time.[21]

Racial tension also played a part in the decline of discipline in Vietnam. Although blacks and whites were united by common needs during combat, the story was different in rear areas where race relations were sometimes poor. Some black soldiers viewed the military as a racist institution and saw Vietnam as a white man's war.[22] This belief, combined with their experience of discrimination in the United States, made some black soldiers suspicious of the mostly white officer and noncommissioned officer corps. They also resented the attempts of Army leaders to prohibit, as contrary to good order and discipline, expressions of racial pride, such as black bootlace jewelry and neck chains, "Afro" haircuts, and "dapping," a racial salute involving a series of mirrored, uniform motions. Sometimes racial unrest escalated into violence. Although most brawls involved only a few soldiers, there were some major confrontations. In 1968, more than 200 black prisoners rioted at Long Binh jail, and in 1970, there was a race riot at Camp Baxter in Da Nang. Friction between the races continued.[23] Years later, one judge advocate observed that major contributing factors in the deterioration of discipline and the complementary challenges to authority were the unpopularity of the war, the perception that black soldiers were disproportionately represented in the combat arms, and racial dissent in the United States.[24]

The breakdown in discipline was reflected in "combat refusals," the official term for disobedience of orders to fight. Although most refusals involved individuals, on at least two occasions company-size units resisted lawful orders. In September 1969, a company of the 196th Light Infantry Brigade refused to recover bodies from a downed helicopter, and in April 1970, CBS Evening News reported the reluctance of a company in the 1st Cavalry Division to advance down a dangerous trail.[25] The most serious mutinous activity, however, was not the combat refusal. Rather, it was the killing or attempted killing of officers and noncommissioned officers. Called "fragging," slang derived from the use of fragmentary grenades, it was carried out by soldiers against unpopular or overly aggressive leaders. Because most fraggings, or "assaults with explosives" as they were officially called, resulted in injury rather than death, the Army concluded that "in the majority of cases the intent is to intimidate or to scare." Nonetheless, with 209 reported fraggings in Vietnam in 1970, some resulting in death, and with similar attacks continuing over the next two years, Army leaders looked to the military justice system for a solution.[26] During his year at U.S. Army Support Command, Qui Nhon, from September 1969 to September 1970, Capt. John T. Edwards prosecuted "maybe six cases of fraggings." There were similar murders or attempted murders during Maj. Leroy F. Foreman's tenure as deputy staff judge advocate of XXIV Corps from June 1969 to June 1970, but involving Claymore mines rather than grenades, the former being "easier to rig." And Capt. Kenneth D. Gray, at U.S. Army Support Command in Da Nang from August 1970 to August 1971, successfully defended a soldier charged with attempting to murder his company commander by placing a grenade under the "hooch" where the officer lived. Probably all judge advocates serving as trial and defense counsel participated in, or knew of, general courts-martial arising out of fragging incidents.[27]

Given the Army's disciplinary problems, a number of prominent figures concluded that the Uniform Code did not work well in combat. Writing in 1980 after the war, Generals Westmoreland and Prugh remarked that the military criminal justice system "is too slow, too cumbersome, too uncertain, too indecisive, and lacking in the power to reinforce accomplishment of the military mission."[28] These words echoed the views of many commanders, who felt that the system had become "too permissive and overzealous in guarding the rights of individuals," to the detriment of discipline.[29] Westmoreland and Prugh proposed correcting the code's shortcomings with a "special codal provision" that would modify the Uniform Code in time of war or military exigency to create a new "Code in Combat."[30]

Questions in high places about the Uniform Code's effectiveness meant that the system of justice was ripe for scrutiny. In 1983 Judge Advocate General Maj. Gen. Hugh J. Clausen, who had served in Vietnam as the staff judge advocate at the 1st Infantry Division, appointed a Wartime Legislation Team of Army lawyers to evaluate the criminal justice system and recommend wartime improvements. The team's report concluded that "although the current system will work with reasonable efficiency during a short, low intensity conflict, several changes are necessary in order to be confident that the system will operate efficiently during a general war."[31] Recommendations, many of them prefigured by Westmoreland and Prugh, included amending the Uniform Code to provide for courts-martial jurisdiction over civilian employees accompanying the forces in time of "declared or undeclared war," to allow misconduct discovered during a pretrial investigation conducted under Article 32 to be charged without a new investigation, and to increase the commanders' punitive powers in imposing nonjudicial punishment under Article 15. The Wartime Legislation Team also proposed amending the Manual for Courts-Martial to allow the substitution of videotape or audiotape recordings of court proceedings for a written record of trial and to permit the investigating officer at an Article 32 investigation to consider the unsworn statements of unavailable witnesses.[32] A number of the team's recommendations were enacted by Congress or implemented by the president. Congress amended the Uniform Code in 1983 so that the term "record" would include both written transcripts and videotape or audiotapes. It also amended the code in 1995 to allow misconduct discovered during an Article 32 investigation to be charged without a new investigation. It is noteworthy that in making these changes Congress did not distinguish between courts-martial in peace or war. This rejection of the call for a special criminal law system for combat reflected the view that transitioning from peace to war should be accomplished with as little change as possible. Military justice, it was concluded, would function less efficiently if commanders and lawyers familiar with one set of rules had to learn new and unfamiliar procedures while preoccupied with combat operations.

Claims

With the Army having single-service responsibility for processing claims in favor of or against U.S. forces in Vietnam, claims remained a significant part of USARV legal operations after 1970. As claims payable to Americans under the Military Personnel Claims Act were handled by unit claims officers, almost all work done by USARV claims lawyers at the USARV Foreign Claims Division involved claims filed by Vietnamese or other foreign nationals. These claims for personal injury, death, or property damage caused by military or civilian members of the U.S. forces resulted from both combat and noncombat damage. As U.S. law forbids paying compensation for combat-related damage, and as the Vietnamese government was responsible for paying all claims arising from the combat activities of American forces, USARV lawyers adjudicated only noncombat claims. Vietnamese claimants, however, still initially looked to the United States for compensation and, as 70 to 90 percent of the total processing time in a foreign claim was spent investigating it, USARV claims officials often discovered that a claim being processed as noncombat-related was in fact the result of combat. This meant that USARV Foreign Claims Division regularly cooperated with the different agencies within the Saigon government responsible for the payment of such claims under the Military Civic Action Program.[33]

By January 1970, the USARV Foreign Claims Division operated two three-man foreign claims commissions with approval authority for claims up to $15,000. Located in downtown Saigon, one commission processed only those claims arising out of an April 1969 explosion at the Da Nang ammunition supply point. Extensive damage to civilian property from the explosion resulted in some 9,000 claims being filed by November 1971. Some were fraudulent and others were untimely, but all had to be processed.[34] The other three-person commission processed the routine workload received from the field at a rate of about 225 claims per month; all cases that could not be settled by a one-man commission in an amount of $1,000 or less were forwarded to this commission. The unusual case that exceeded the jurisdiction of this three-man commission would be forwarded to the Pentagon for a decision by the assistant secretary of the Army (financial management).[35]

In addition to the two three-man commissions, twelve one-man foreign claims commissions, with approval authority for claims up to $1,000, also operated in Vietnam. Five were located in Saigon. The remaining seven were in Da Nang (with XXIV Corps), Phuoc Vinh (with the 1st Cavalry Division), Qui Nhon (with the U.S. Army Support Command), Nha Trang (with I Field Force), Chu Lai (with the 23d Infantry Division), and two one-man commissions at Camp Eagle near Hue (with the 101st Airborne Division). In 1970 and 1971, these twelve one-person commissions processed about 2,000 claims per year. In 1972, as the American presence dwindled, the number of claims filed by Vietnamese nationals also declined, as did the number of one-man commissions. USARV Foreign Claims Division, however, remained in operation until 1973.[36]

During these final years of lawyering in Vietnam, USARV claims judge advocates looked for solutions to three major questions. First, should compensation be paid for combat-related damage or loss based on the reckless and wanton conduct of U.S. forces? Second, who should have claims responsibility upon complete withdrawal of U.S. forces from Vietnam? Finally, what should be done about increasingly violent Vietnamese-U.S. confrontations over claims for damage or loss?

Under U.S. law, appropriated monies could not be used to compensate for combat-related damage or loss of life. The nature of the war in Vietnam, however, meant that this prohibition seemed unfair. The battlefield was anywhere and everywhere, with no identifiable front lines and no safe area. This meant that innocent civilians could not easily avoid the war or its suffering. Recognizing that compensation for losses relating to the combat activities of U.S. forces could not be paid under the Foreign Claims Act, but believing that this position was wrong given the nature of the fighting, MACV decided that its Assistance-in-Kind funds would be used to pay for some combat-related damage. As a result, the USARV Foreign Claims Division processed Vietnamese claims springing indirectly from combat if the loss or damage was caused by reckless or wanton conduct by U.S. forces. While injuries resulting from a firefight between U.S. troops and guerrilla forces were not compensable, loss of life or damage to property caused by a soldier on patrol who indiscriminately fired his weapon into a village was compensable. Paying these claims demonstrated that the Americans took responsibility for their own behavior, showed the Vietnamese people that the law could confer a benefit, and, it was hoped, fostered popular respect for law in Vietnam.[37]

Who should have claims responsibility upon complete withdrawal of U.S. forces from Vietnam? As early as October 1971, Maj. Ralph G. Miranda, chief of the Foreign Claims Division, recommended to the USARV staff judge advocate that a plan be formulated for processing foreign claims submitted after U.S. forces departed. Miranda anticipated that Vietnamese nationals would continue filing claims then handled by the USARV Foreign Claims Division. He also believed that when departing U.S. forces returned leased real properties prior to the expiration of the leases, Vietnamese landlords would file substantial claims against the United States. Maj. Miranda anticipated that as U.S. troop strength decreased and various support agencies terminated operations, the need for local national employees would diminish, resulting in claims for termination pay.[38] Finally, there would also be claims arising out of contracts with Vietnamese businesses for goods or services. After coordination with MACV and the Air Force and Navy, it was decided that the Army would continue foreign claims processing at U.S. Army, Pacific. Thus, until 1975, foreign claims were accepted at the Defense Attaché Office in Saigon and by the U.S. consular staff throughout South Vietnam and then forwarded for action to Army headquarters in Hawaii.[39]

The third claims issue of personal interest to claims judge advocates was what could be done "to cool off potentially explosive situations" involving claims for loss or damage. After 1970, as the Vietnamese saw American units departing and as the backlog of claims cases increased, one lieutenant general reported that "they visualize that the only means of getting a prompt and adequate settlement is via the confrontation approach."[40] On one occasion, several hundred Vietnamese claimants blocked the entrance to a U.S. military compound in the XXIV Corps area, refusing to leave until their claims were paid. The disturbance was quelled only after the chief of the USARV Foreign Claims Division flew from Saigon to Da Nang, met personally with the village and hamlet chiefs, and assured them that "we would do all within our power to settle the problem as soon as possible."[41]

The danger posed to claims commissioners by these confrontations was illustrated by the experiences of Capt. Donald A. Deline, the Da Nang claims commissioner from May to September 1970. Arriving in Vietnam in September 1969, Deline first served in Saigon at the USARV claims office, processing mostly foreign claims. In May, he was reassigned to Da Nang as a one-man claims commissioner. Foreign claims work was additional duty for all seven one-man commissioners located outside Saigon except in Deline's Da Nang operation, which processed about one-half of the 1,000 claims handled by the one-man commissions. Da Nang's heavier volume resulted from an April 1969 ammunition supply point explosion that caused extensive damage to civilian property and formed the basis for some 5,000 claims over the next two years.[42]

Capt. Deline's offices were in a villa in downtown Da Nang, and Vietnamese citizens came there during the day, filed their claims, and were told when to return for payment in Vietnamese piasters. Typically Deline picked up the money from the XXIV Corps finance office, returned with it under guard to his office, and paid out exactly what he had picked up. But it was not always this simple. One night in May 1970, a Vietnamese Army officer riding a motorcycle was struck by an American military truck. A number of his fellow soldiers surrounded the vehicle, refusing to let the American driver leave until the victim had been compensated for the damage to his motorcycle. Although it was 2200, Deline traveled to the accident, took photographs, and, working with the Vietnamese officer victim, completed the claims forms that evening. The unit commander with responsibility for the American truck and driver wanted Deline to pay the victim's claim immediately, but Deline resisted, believing that any claim for damages should go through the normal deliberative process.[43]

A week later a 2 1/2-ton Marine Corps truck struck and killed a young Vietnamese boy. Knowing that confrontation had brought good results for the motorcycle victim, a crowd of more than a hundred Vietnamese surrounded the truck containing the marines and refused to let it leave. The Marines requested that Capt. Deline go to the accident scene. Arriving with some claims forms in his old International Harvester truck, Deline discovered that concertina wire had been placed around the Marine Corps truck. The dead child was lying on an altar in front of the truck, and the boy's mother and others were praying loudly. Some South Vietnamese Army soldiers were also on the scene and they, together with the local mayor, informed Deline that they wanted money. About 2300, a Marine Corps officer appeared at the scene. After making a small solatia payment to the victim's family, he and Deline started to leave the house in which the discussions had been taking place. Although armed with a .45-caliber pistol, Deline was held down in his chair; the Marine officer was escorted out.

For the next two to three very tense hours, Capt. Deline and the Marines in the truck remained captive. Then, about 0200, a Marine Corps colonel arrived by jeep with $3,000 to $5,000 in Vietnamese piasters. This was his own money. The colonel laid it on the table. The piasters were sufficient for the crowd to permit the colonel and the Marines in the truck to drive away, leaving Deline by himself. The Marine colonel returned his men to their barracks and then sent two military policemen back for Deline, who was still being held hostage. By now it was 0400; Deline did not know if he and the police "should push our way out or not." Finally, they did force their way out of the house and, although the Vietnamese were yelling angrily and striking the three Americans, Deline and the two military policemen escaped.[44]

Military Affairs

In the area of military affairs, USARV judge advocates provided command advice on administrative law matters. Most work involved advising on and later reviewing reports of investigation and elimination of soldiers through the administrative discharge process. For example, a war crime would be reported, USARV headquarters would appoint a

94

lieutenant colonel investigating officer, and the military affairs judge advocates would show the investigating officer how to conduct the investigation. After the report was completed, another lawyer would review it for legal sufficiency and appropriate recommendations. One of the most celebrated investigations reviewed by USARV lawyers, however, did not involve any war crime. Rather, it concerned the attack by enemy sappers on Fire Support Base MARY ANN, an Americal Division outpost up in I Corps.

In March 1971, a group of between fifty and sixty well-prepared enemy penetrated MARY ANN's perimeter and, tossing grenades and satchel charges into the tactical operations center, killed or wounded virtually all of the base's officers. An investigation concluded that the failure of the officers in charge to post guards or follow other proper defensive procedures was grossly negligent and contributed directly to the heavy American casualties—thirty dead and eighty-two wounded.[45] Maj. Suter, newly assigned to the USARV staff judge advocate's office, was tasked with reviewing the MARY ANN investigation, fixing responsibility for the disaster, and recommending an appropriate course of action. After digesting the classified report's eleven volumes, Suter briefed Lt. Gen. William J. McCaffrey, the USARV deputy commander. Suter recommended no courts-martial, but urged reprimands, administrative elimination action, and adverse efficiency reports. McCaffrey approved all recommendations.[46]

Later, while serving as chief of the Civil Law Division, Maj. Suter spearheaded the creation of USARV's Drug Abuser Holding Center. In response to Lt. Gen. McCaffrey's demand that "something" be done about soldier drug addicts, the USARV staff judge advocate created a regulation transferring "all second time drug abusers" from any subordinate USARV unit to the new holding center. Although located in the old Long Binh jail, the center was not a confinement building, but rather, as indicated by the freshly painted red cross on the side of the structure, a medical facility. It housed soldiers needing treatment for drug addiction until they could be administratively eliminated from the Army and "medically evacuated" for treatment in the United States at a Veterans Administration hospital. As any soldier arriving at the facility was informed that he would receive either an honorable or a general discharge, almost all waived the right to have a board of officers hear the case. Under Suter's supervision, the two judge advocates there, working in tandem as recorder for the government and counsel for the respondent, processed "1,500 soldiers in six months."[47] The Drug Abuser Holding Center was a novel and efficient method for eliminating soldiers whose drug addiction made treatment seem more appropriate than punishment by courts-martial.

Lawyering in the Field

Until the last combat units left in 1972, judge advocates lawyered actively and effectively with them. The experiences of military attorneys at the 1st Cavalry, 25th Infantry, and 101st Airborne Divisions illustrate lawyering in Vietnam in the final years.

1st Cavalry Division

Roughly forty judge advocates served with the 1st Cavalry Division in Vietnam. Its first staff judge advocate, Lt. Col. Morris D. Hodges, was followed by Lt. Cols. Emory M. Sneeden and Zane E. Finkelstein, Maj. Sebert L. Trail, and Lt. Col. Bryan S. Spencer. By 1970, Lt. Col. Ronald M. Holdaway was the staff judge advocate, and although the division's table of organization and equipment authorized five attorneys, Holdaway had about fifteen lawyers.

Lt. Col. Holdaway and his attorneys were at the division's main headquarters at Phuoc Vinh, where about 500 troops worked and lived

Life at the 1st Air Cavalry Division, Camp Evans, South Vietnam (1968). From left to right are: Chief Warrant Officer Daniel P. Koceja; Capt. Carroll J. Tichenor; and Maj. Sebert L. Trail. Trail was the division's staff judge advocate from 1968 to 1969.

in Spartan conditions. As a principal staff officer, Holdaway had better accommodations than most; his cot was in a former French Foreign Legion building located on the Phuoc Vinh compound. The JAG office and living accommodations for the junior officers and enlisted personnel were at a rubber plantation about 400 meters from the compound. The buildings were so-called SEAHUTS (Southeast Asia Huts) erected as temporary structures. There was no running water and the latrines were outdoors. Enemy rocket attacks occurred frequently, so most attorneys sandbagged their living areas for additional protection. Every few weeks the 1st Cavalry Division's lawyers would wake to discover Viet Cong sappers caught in the concertina wire surrounding the camp; living and working in Phuoc Vinh was not without risk.[48]

Lawyering at the 1st Cavalry Division was different from practicing law at other combat units. The division had been in almost continuous combat since arriving in Vietnam in September 1965, and this meant, in Lt. Col. Holdaway's view, that although commanders "took their military justice roles very seriously . . . it was a distraction from their fighting mission." Consequently, a commander taking action in a particular criminal case wanted his judge advocate to summarize the case very briefly and recommend a decision or specific course of action. This way a heavy caseload could be disposed of quite efficiently. As Holdaway remembered, a lawyer who did not or could not provide terse and specific recommendations lost the trust and confidence of his commander.[49]

The 1st Cavalry's airmobility posed challenges for the lawyers. With about 450 helicopters, the division was not dependent on ground transport for movement, either tactically or administratively. This meant that the 1st Cavalry had a very large area of operations and that its firebases were located at great distances from headquarters where roads did not go. In 1970, with all the lawyers located at the division main headquarters, such activities as interviewing witnesses for trial, advising convening authorities located outside of Phuoc Vinh, and in some instances actively conducting trials at firebases required traveling by air. Additionally, troops normally did not come into headquarters for personal legal assistance or to file claims; judge advocates brought legal services to them. Consequently, "the MO [Method of Operation] for young counsel was to go down and hang around the helicopter pad and hitch rides out to the firebases." Once airborne, he still had a half hour to an hour flight, no matter where he went. In addition to the young captains, Lt. Col. Holdaway was typically airborne, often flying out to base camps and firebases to confer with and advise commanders. As a principal staff officer, he was normally able to obtain a helicopter for all his lawyerly missions. So, too, before long, were his juniors-thanks to the division chief of staff, Col. (later Gen.) Edward C. Meyer, a helicopter was dedicated one-half day a week for use by the Army lawyers. It was known as the "lawbird" on the days it flew.[50]

1st Air Cavalry Division, January 1970. Left: Major Walter M. Mayer, Deputy Staff Judge Advocate; and Right: Lieutenant Colonel Ronald M. Holdaway, Staff Judge Advocate. During Holdaway's tenure, the 1st Cavalry lawyers were often airborne. They flew out to base camps and firebases to confer with and advise commanders and bring legal services to soldiers who needed them.

Army lawyers provided the full range of legal services during Holdaway's tenure, with military justice occupying most attorney time. One of the attorneys trying courts-martial was Capt. Royce C. Lamberth. After graduating from law school in 1967, Lamberth was drafted into the infantry. Once he finished basic training, however, he accepted a direct commission in the Judge Advocate General's Corps. Lamberth served briefly as a judge advocate at XVIII Airborne Corps at Fort Bragg before arriving at Phuoc Vinh in November 1969. He immediately assumed a heavy courts-martial caseload, serving as both a prosecutor and a defense counsel. While the general courts-martial were tried at division headquarters, the inferior courts-martial were often tried at the brigade bases because the commanders did not want witnesses "leaving the field." Consequently, Lamberth, accompanied by the military judge and his opposing counsel, routinely flew in a small unarmed observation helicopter out to these bases for the trials. Proceedings were typically held in a tent.[51]

During his year in Vietnam, Capt. Lamberth tried more than 200 cases. The most memorable involved defending a team of six Rangers accused of mutilating the bodies of enemy soldiers. The Rangers had ambushed some North Vietnamese soldiers bicycling down the "Jolley Trail," a major infiltration route into South Vietnam. One or more of the Rangers later boasted over a few beers that, after killing the enemy soldiers, they had "cut open the bodies from throat to groin and stuffed them with rice" from the 100-pound burlap bags strapped to the enemy bicycles. This "calling card" was intended to strike fear into any enemy who later happened upon the dead men.

The Rangers, however, soon regretted telling their war story, as their alleged mutilation of the dead was reported as a war crime. A lieutenant colonel with the MACV inspector general's office arrived at the 1st Cavalry Division to interview the six Rangers. Each man had the same story to tell: they had ambushed and killed the enemy but no mutilation of the dead had occurred; that had just been bragging. After reducing their statements to writing, the investigator asked the six Rangers to submit to a polygraph. They balked. All asked for a lawyer, and Lamberth was assigned to represent all six men. With his clients facing courts-martial, Lamberth filed a motion requesting that Maj. Gen. Elvy B. Roberts, the division commander, "produce" the bodies of the dead North Vietnamese. He argued that only if the bodies were produced would the six Americans "be able to establish their innocence." After a late night staff meeting that included the chief of staff and the G3 (operations), the commanding general decided it would be consistent with planned operations in the area to send an aerial rifle platoon to search for the bodies. Lt. Col. Holdaway insisted that the defense counsel go on the mission to ensure there would be no later claim of a cover-up. Holdaway then told Lamberth that he was departing by helicopter at first light.[52]

Air Force jets and Cobra helicopter gunships "prepped" the insertion site for the Huey utility helicopter, or "Slick," carrying Lamberth and the six Rangers. Then, about 100 feet above the bomb crater where the insertion was to occur, the engine quit. The helicopter crashed. Assuming that they were shot down, Lamberth, the only officer aboard other than the warrant officer pilot, and the Rangers "fired like hell" from their perimeter into the jungle. When no fire was returned, the men realized that mechanical failure caused the crash. They radioed for a Sky Crane helicopter to recover the crashed aircraft and for a new "Slick" to pick them up. Meanwhile, Capt. Lamberth and the Rangers walked the Jolley Trail. They found the bicycles, burlap bags containing rice, and lots of blood. One soldier found an enemy bunker, which was blown up with hand grenades. A bridge along the trail was also destroyed. But there were no bodies, which really came as no surprise to the six Rangers. Lamberth and his clients returned without further incident. In the absence of corroborative evidence, no courts-martial charges were preferred. After the events of Lamberth's trip become known, however, other soldiers facing courts-martial charges requested him as their individual military defense counsel; "the word got around" that this lawyer "would do anything for a client."[53]

25th Infantry Division

Between 1966 when the division arrived and 1970 when its colors left Vietnam for Hawaii, some twenty-five judge advocates served with the "Tropic Lightning" Division. The first staff judge advocate was Lt. Col. David T. Bryant. Following him were Lt. Cols. William A. Ziegler and Jack Norton and Maj. Fred Bright, Jr. Official personnel records show that the number of judge advocates at the division during this period varied from six in 1967 to ten in 1970. But as U.S. Army, Vietnam, continued supplementing the division's legal operations with attorneys serving in other branches, the legal workload in the 25th was also borne by lawyers other than those in the Judge Advocate General's Corps.

The last staff judge advocate in Vietnam with the 25th Infantry Division was Maj. Burnett H. Radosh, who arrived at division headquarters at Cu Chi in January 1970. He had a legal staff of ten judge advocates, plus one non-judge advocate lawyer. Radosh, who had served as a captain with Col. Miller at 1st Logistical Command in 1966, now was back for his second twelve-month tour in Vietnam as the top

Maj. Gen. Kenneth J. Hodson (center) visits Lt. Col. Fred J. Bright, Jr. (left) and Maj. Richard K. Dahlinger (right) at the 25th Infantry Division, Cu Chi, Vietnam, in 1969. Bright was the division's staff judge advocate and Dahlinger was the deputy staff judge advocate.

lawyer on the division staff. Drafted after completing law school in 1958, Radosh spent a short time as a Courts and Boards clerk before receiving a direct appointment in the Judge Advocate General's Corps in 1959. He then served in the Defense Appellate Division in the Pentagon; in the 1st, 3d, and 4th Logistical Commands in France; and in the 82d Airborne Division, deploying for a short time with the division to the Dominican Republic in 1965. After his first tour in Vietnam, Radosh worked as a trial attorney at Contract Appeals Division in the Office of the Judge Advocate General. When he arrived for his second Vietnam tour in January 1970, Radosh was well prepared for duty.

Radosh and his attorneys "had a horrible workload at the 25th-stacks and stacks of courts-martial." There were hundreds of claims for damaged property from soldiers and much legal assistance work to be done, from replying to divorce petitions to drafting stays in civil proceedings using the Soldiers' and Sailors' Civil Relief Act. The "Tropic Lightning" lawyers also gave regular talks to division soldiers on their obligations under the Law of War. The volume of work was so great that Maj. Radosh, Deputy Staff Judge Advocate Maj. Richard K. Dahlinger, and nine lawyers, assisted by ten enlisted soldiers, worked six days a week, twelve hours a day. Sunday usually was a "day off," but often work had to be done that day, too. As the 25th had been at Cu Chi since 1966, living conditions were fairly good. Radosh, for example, lived in a hut with a tin roof. Although not air-conditioned, this "hootch" was comfortable.

Although the practice of law was fairly routine, there were always interesting legal questions. At an evening staff meeting, for example, Maj. Radosh heard a briefer inform the division commander that a Viet Cong prisoner had been used to lead troops through a minefield. Radosh waited until the meeting ended, then told the commander and the chief of staff that nothing could be more illegal under the Law of War. On another occasion, prior to the 25th's movement across the border into Cambodia, Radosh inquired of Col. Williams, the MACV staff judge advocate, what the legal status of U.S. forces would be once inside Cambodia. Williams pointed to a map of Southeast Asia and said, "as you advance the border advances." That is, under traditional international law, troops in combat are governed by the law of the flag; in the absence of a Status of Forces Agreement with Cambodia, U.S. law governed the activities of American troops in that country.[54]

One of the judge advocates at the 25th Infantry Division was Capt. Howard R. Andrews, Jr. Having arrived in Vietnam as an enlisted field artilleryman, Andrews, who was also an attorney, served several months in fire direction centers in the 101st Airborne Division before moving to that division's legal operations. After receiving a direct commission in the Judge Advocate General's Corps, Andrews transferred to the 25th Infantry in January 1970. Over the next three months, he served at the 25th's Cu Chi base camp, worked as chief of international law, and also prosecuted and defended at courts-martial. On 17 April 1970, Andrews flew by helicopter to the Long Binh stockade to see a client who had recently been court-martialed. After seeing this man, Andrews was invited to remain at Long Binh for a party in honor of a fellow lawyer departing for the United States after a year in Vietnam. Andrews, however, "had seven cases on his docket and much to do"; he decided instead to return to Cu Chi. He boarded a regularly scheduled courier helicopter about 1800. Shortly after takeoff, the helicopter struck a power line and crashed into the river. Andrews and several others were killed. This accident gave Andrews the unwanted distinction of being the only judge advocate killed in Vietnam.[55]

101st Airborne Division

By 1970, the 101st's main headquarters was at Camp Eagle outside Phu Bai, and its staff judge advocate was Lt. Col. Carl Wellborn. Wellborn, who enjoyed supplementing his legal work with missions as a helicopter door gunner, had some seven judge advocates on his staff. One of the newest was Capt. Benjamin H. White.

White, an ex-Medical Service Corps officer, had transferred to the Judge Advocate General's Corps in 1969. After a short stint as an Army lawyer at Fort Stewart, Georgia, Capt. White attended the Judge Advocate Officer Basic Course in Charlottesville, Virginia. From there, he flew to Long Binh via Hawaii and Guam, finally arriving at Camp Eagle in June 1970. A large compound having some 20,000 personnel, Camp Eagle was "about a mile wide and five miles long." Both division and support troops lived and worked there. For White, the first order of business was finding a bunk and some jungle fatigues that would fit him. After this, it was getting acclimated to conditions. "It was hotter than hell ... the office had metal desks and you put a towel on the desk if you wanted to lean on it otherwise you would burn yourself." At night it got down to 90 degrees. There was no air-conditioning; an electric fan was all that was available. When the monsoon season started the first week of October, this meant wet and cool weather. There was so much rain that "everything was wet ... from October to March the sun only came out about five times." An electric light bulb in the ammunition box he used for storage kept things dry, and White also kept his electric blanket on all day to keep his bunk dry. Off-duty hours were spent playing foosball in the officers' club, reading, writing letters, playing chess, and drinking beer.[56]

For the first six months there, working ten to twelve hours a day, seven days a week, Capt. White did both prosecution and defense work. He was the trial counsel for one special court-martial jurisdiction, prosecuting all special courts and general courts arising in that unit. White was the defense counsel for all court cases coming out of the division's three brigades, division artillery, and aviation group. Courts-martial ranged from murder and rape to drug abuse and disobedience of orders. It was not unusual to prosecute a jury case during daylight hours and, after the court-martial panel had recessed for the day, to prosecute and defend judge-alone courts-martial into the evening. Additionally, on more than one occasion the military judge recessed the court proceedings because of incoming enemy rocket fire.[57]

At the end of his first six months, Capt. White was given the option of leaving the 101st for a "safer" assignment in the Saigon or Long Binh area. He decided, however, that he liked where he was; "the camaraderie was really great." His seniority now meant he was the chief of military affairs as well as a one-man foreign claims commissioner. This meant reviewing reports of survey and reports of investigation. It also meant traveling by jeep into the countryside with his Vietnamese interpreter, paying claims. The typical claim was for maneuver damage to farmland, but there also were payments to Vietnamese who had been injured by 101st Airborne Division vehicles.[58]

The Last Army Lawyers
U.S. Army, Vietnam/Military Assistance Command, Vietnam

With the withdrawal of the 3d Brigade of the 1st Cavalry Division in June 1972, the American combat troop presence was at an end. Although Troop F, 4th Cavalry, remained in the Saigon area as a protective force, there was no longer a need for a separate Army headquarters. USARV headquarters and the Long Binh facilities closed, and a new unit, U.S. Army, Vietnam/Military Assistance Command, Vietnam, emerged in October 1972. Initially, Col. Tenhet, the new USARV/MACV staff judge advocate, and the twenty-two judge advocates under his supervision at Tan Son Nhut continued the traditional legal business of prosecuting and defending courts-martial, processing claims, providing legal assistance, and advising commanders and staffs.

The 27 January 1973 signing of the Paris Agreement on Ending the War and Restoring Peace in Vietnam, however, radically altered business for USARV/MACV lawyers. Because the United States had committed itself to withdrawing all its troops within sixty days, judge advocates now had a two-month "roll-up phase" for all legal operations, including winding up programs like those at the Advisory Division that had existed for more than ten years. At the same time, Army lawyers faced a new challenge in helping with the orderly implementation of the Paris Peace Accords, including monitoring the cease-fire and accounting for Americans held as prisoners of war or missing in action. In short, rather than decreasing, legal work for the USARV/MACV lawyers increased during February and March. The judge advocates did their best in the chaos, but "trying to get organized in a withdrawing Army was exceedingly difficult."[59]

The plan was for complete legal services to be provided in the "standdown phase" from "X," the date of the agreement, to "X plus 35 days." During the "withdrawal phase" from X plus 35 until X plus 59, trials of courts-martial, adjudication and approval of Military Personnel Claims, routine legal assistance, and formal administrative law opinions were curtailed, except in urgent situations. After X plus 59, all judge advocate activities were completed or transferred to other jurisdictions. Although there was "no insurmountable obstacle . . . in providing legal support to the withdrawing Army," USARV/MACV legal operations suffered most from a loss of manpower. Lawyers were needed to resolve expected and unexpected legal issues until X plus 59, yet judge advocates were returning to the United States without replacement.[60]

Military Justice

The challenge for USARV/MACV military justice practitioners was cleaning up courts-martial actions left by departing units while keeping up with the ongoing caseload. When Capt. Dennis M. Corrigan arrived in Saigon in August 1972, Maj. Robert E. Murray, the USARV/MACV chief of justice, showed him "a 20 by 15 foot room, full of tapes, exhibits, and uncompleted records," some of which were more than a year old. The 1st Cavalry Division alone had left 160 general courts-martial unfinished, all requiring the creation of a verbatim record of trial by transcribing hundreds of tapes of recorded testimony. At the same time, the haphazard manner in which general court proceedings had been left behind by withdrawing units created significant problems. For example, although the accused had been convicted of a charge, on more than one occasion that charge had to be dismissed because in doing the posttrial review for convening authority action, the supporting evidence was nowhere to be found. A soldier convicted of selling heroin had the case against him dismissed because the exhibit identified as the lab report was missing.[61]

Corrigan and Murray also had to keep up with the current caseload. Though USARV/MACV headquarters was the only remaining general court-martial convening authority in Vietnam after the departure of 1st Cavalry Division's 3d Brigade, all serious criminal misconduct required prosecution by lawyers from Saigon traveling around the country. With some 120 courts—martial on the docket at any one time, judge advocates tried cases seven days a week. More than half the general court caseload involved drugs, mostly heroin use and sale. Guard offenses—sleeping on guard duty, leaving guard duty, incapacitated for guard duty—were also prosecuted at general courts-martial. Of course, USARV/MACV judge advocates also tried and defended cases involving murders, rapes, robberies, and serious assaults.

The withdrawal of U.S. forces, however, complicated even small administrative matters. General court-martial convening orders, for example, needed frequent amendments as court members departed Vietnam for the United States. The chief obstacle for prosecutors, however, was that under the terms of the Paris Peace Accords, as interpreted by the Department of State, it was no longer possible to bring witnesses back to Vietnam for any trials. More than a few serious crimes could not be prosecuted because a witness present in the United States, even if willing to return to Vietnam, could not do so. In January 1973 Capt. Corrigan prosecuted a MACV master sergeant who had shot a Vietnamese woman in his barracks room a few months earlier. The woman, shot through her cheek and neck, claimed that the accused had held her on her knees with a pistol to her head to force her to perform a sex act. The accused claimed he and the victim had struggled while standing when she grabbed a $20 bill from his nightstand, and his pistol had "gone off." Critical to the government's case was the testimony of the MACV Support Command dentist who, having examined the victim's mouth, was prepared to testify that the shooting was no accident. The dentist, however, had already shipped to Hawaii and, having departed Vietnam, could no longer return under the terms of the Paris Peace Accords.[62]

Not surprisingly, the after-action report authored by Maj. Murray and Capt. Corrigan advised that procedures be created to effect an orderly handoff of cases during any future withdrawal. Earlier, as units had inactivated or redeployed, they had handed their cases off to other units. But at the end, when the troop units were gone, the remaining cases ended up with USARV/MACV judge advocates, who lacked the resources to deal with them. As it was, Murray tasked a senior noncommissioned officer and nine to ten court reporters with transcribing the tape-recorded proceedings of the court cases left behind by the 1st Cavalry Division. It took several months to eliminate the backlog. Corrigan and Murray also recommended that "legislative or Manual for Courts-Martial changes" be made, "easing the rules for use of depositions or creating other alternatives to returning witnesses during a withdrawal."[63]

Despite the chaos of lawyering in the last few months, military justice functioned relatively well until the end. In March 1973, when Capt. Corrigan, accompanied by a court reporter and legal clerk, left Vietnam, he was manacled to the last prisoner from the Long Binh jail. Arriving in Hawaii by airplane, Corrigan turned the accused over to the 25th Infantry Division at Schofield Barracks. That division had the distinction of prosecuting the last court-martial from Vietnam.[64]

Administrative Law, Legal Assistance, International Law, and Claims

USARV/MACV judge advocates continued providing complete legal services in all areas, but after the signing of the Paris Peace Accords, functions were ranked in order of importance. Administrative law continued, but expertise at the action-officer level was lost with the departure of experienced lawyers after X plus 10. Although plans called for legal assistance on an emergency basis only, USARV/MACV lawyers were able to give advice when needed by military and civilian personnel. The Defense Attaché Office legal adviser agreed to provide legal assistance for those eligible personnel remaining in Vietnam at the end of the withdrawal.[65]

Claims payable under either the Military Personnel Claims Act or the Foreign Claims Act were adjudicated until the middle of March 1973. After discontinuing operations, the USARV Claims Office forwarded its remaining 100 military personnel claims to U.S. Army,

Pacific, for action. Additionally, the Defense Attaché Office agreed to accept future claims and to forward them to Hawaii for adjudication. Similarly, while continuing to process noncombat claims filed by Vietnamese and other foreign nationals, Maj. James A. Murphy, chief of the Foreign Claims Division, arranged for the Defense Attaché Office in Saigon and U.S. consuls general throughout Vietnam to accept future foreign claims for forwarding to a newly created Foreign Claims Commission at U.S. Army, Pacific, for adjudication. All pending foreign claims were transferred to the new commission in mid-March 1973.[66]

Finally, all functional files for USARV/MACV legal operations were boxed and delivered to the USARV adjutant general for shipment to the U.S. Army, Pacific records holding area for retirement. Selected records, however, were air mailed or hand carried by judge advocates to Hawaii when they left Vietnam. Certain administrative law opinions and records of trial in cases pending convening authority action or appellate review fell into this category.[67]

Four-Party Joint Military Commission

On 27 January 1973, the United States, South Vietnam, North Vietnam, and the Provisional Revolutionary Government (or Viet Cong) signed the Agreement on Ending the War and Restoring Peace in Vietnam. This agreement, also known as the Paris Peace Accords, established a cease-fire and required the withdrawal of all remaining American, Australian, New Zealander, and South Korean forces within sixty days. Overseeing this final troop pullout was the Four-Party Joint Military Commission, which was to serve as a forum for

The Paris Peace Accords signed on 27 January 1973 created a Four-Party Joint Military Commission to oversee the implementation of the agreement. The main commission sat in Saigon; seven regional commissions were established throughout the country. Army judge advocate Capt. Arthur F. Lincoln (far right) was an official member on the Region IV commission. To his left are the Chief, North Vietnam Delegation; Chief, Provisional Revolutionary Government (Viet Cong) Delegation; and Chief, Army of the Republic of Vietnam Delegation.

communication among the four parties, assist in the implementation of the agreement, and help verify compliance with it. Additionally, the commission was to arrange the return of prisoners of war and gather information about those missing in action.[68]

As Article 16 of the Paris agreement gave the Joint Military Commission a lifespan of only sixty days, the commission was organized quickly. The four parties agreed that the commission would be headquartered in Saigon and that seven regional joint military commissions would be set up. Military representatives of each of the four parties were appointed for Saigon and for each region. Having decided that Army judge advocates should participate in the work of the Joint Military Commission, Col. Tenhet, the USARV/MACV staff judge advocate, selected Maj. Paul P. Dommer, the incumbent chief of the Advisory Division, as the legal adviser to the U.S. delegation to the central Four-Party Joint Military Commission in Saigon for the sixty days of that organization's life.[69] More junior judge advocates from Tenhet's office were detailed as legal advisers to the regional joint military commissions.[70]

CHỨNG-MINH-THƯ
CREDENTIALS

As a member of the Region IV commission, Capt. Lincoln carried this "credentials" card as proof of this official status. The reverse contains the following language: 'The holder of this card is a member of the Four-Party Joint Military Commission established by the Agreement on Ending the War and Restoring Peace in Vietnam. When implementing the mission entrusted by the Four-Party Joint Military Commission, presentation of this certificate is sufficient and all administrative and military legal authorities are strictly responsible to grant him protection and assistance in every respect as stipulated in the Agreement and its Protocols.'

Capt. Vahan Moushegian, Jr. was one of those selected as a regional joint military commission legal adviser. Arriving in April 1972 as a military intelligence officer, Moushegian worked as a MACV intelligence desk officer for Cambodia and Laos before transferring to the Judge Advocate General's Corps in November 1972. Assigned to the USARV staff judge advocate's office, Moushegian prosecuted

108

special courts-martial under the supervision of Maj. Murray, the USARV chief of justice, until the signing of the Paris Peace Accords. Moushegian then joined the joint military commission in Region V, located in Bien Hoa, north of Saigon. Col. Walter F. Ulmer, the chief of the U.S. delegation, informed Moushegian that he was to be "the delegation's expert on the Paris Peace Accords," and in the formal meetings of the Region V commission that followed Moushegian advised and assisted both Col. Ulmer and the deputy chief of the U.S. delegation. Because Col. Ulmer's Viet Cong counterpart "never came out of the jungle" to represent the Provisional Revolutionary Government, the commission's four deputy chiefs of delegation soon were meeting a few hours every other day around a square table covered with green felt.

In discussing the intent and implementation of the Paris Peace Accords, the participants wrangled constantly over how the provisions should be interpreted; thus, little was achieved at the formal sessions. The meetings ranged from the significant (repatriation of American and South Vietnamese prisoners of war) to the ordinary (the ability of the North Vietnamese and Viet Cong delegations to travel freely throughout Region V) to the absurd (whether the fans at the conference table adequately cooled the attendees). Generally, while the Provisional Revolutionary Government and the North Vietnamese were in agreement and supported each other, the Americans and South Vietnamese were sometimes at odds, making it difficult to present a united front or to pursue a common strategy in the talks. Additionally, as the Paris Peace Accords required any decision reached by the Joint Military Commission to be unanimous, one party's objection blocked any progress.[71]

Capt. Moushegian's role evolved over time to where he also assumed, in addition to his responsibilities as the legal adviser, the duties of principal liaison officer for the U.S. delegation. Thus, when the deputy chiefs of delegation stopped having formal meetings because of a lack of measurable progress, the liaison officers were instructed to meet regularly to ensure there was continued dialogue on the implementation of the Paris Peace Accords. That said, "almost nothing was accomplished by the Joint Military Commission," in Moushegian's view, because "there were only eight weeks [and] the Viet Cong and North Vietnamese would not agree to anything because they knew the United States was leaving Vietnam."[72]

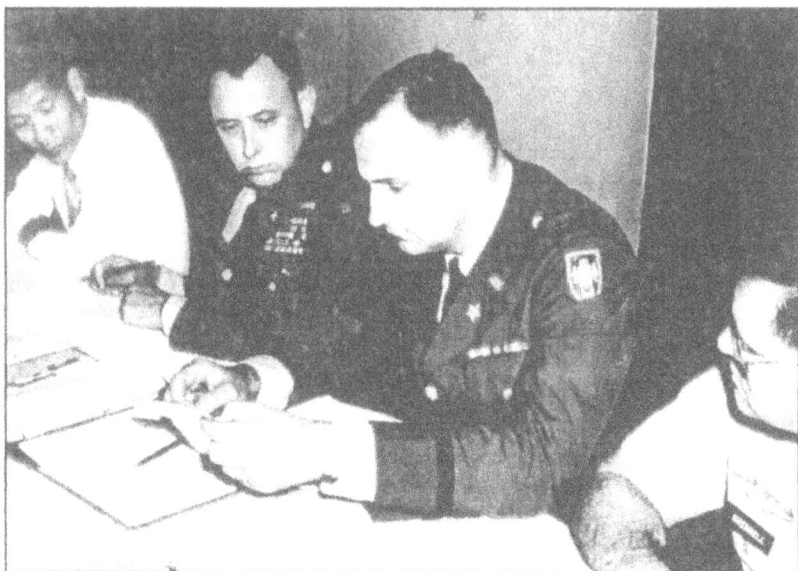

Capt. Jerome W. Scanlon, Jr., legal advisor to the Four-Party Joint Military Team, examines documents provided by the North Vietnamese at a 6 March 1974 meeting in Hanoi. Although a judge advocate, Scanlon wore general staff insignia at the direction of the chief of staff of the U.S. delegation. Scanlon, who served in Vietnam from July 1973 to July 1974, was one of the last military lawyers in Vietnam. He retired as a lieutenant colonel in 1985.

Four-Party Joint Military Team

On 27 March 1973, U.S. Army, Vietnam/Military Assistance Command, Vietnam, dissolved and the last American combat troops left Vietnam. The Four-Party Joint Military Commission also ceased operation, and Maj. Dommer, Capt. Moushegian, and the other judge advocates working with it left for the United States. A new organization, the Four-Party Joint Military Team, now replaced the Joint Military Commission. From the perspective of the U.S. delegation, this new Joint Military Team had two functions: locating and recovering the remains of Americans who had died in captivity and discovering the whereabouts of those still missing in action.

A lone Army lawyer now served in Vietnam, assigned as the legal adviser to the U.S. Delegation to the Joint Military Team. The first legal adviser was Maj. Charles R. Murray, who served with the team from the end of March until the middle of July. His replacement was Capt. Jerome W. Scanlon, Jr. A former field artillery officer with service in Germany, Scanlon transferred to the Judge Advocate General's Corps in 1969. He then served at Fort Dix, New Jersey, and, while attending the Judge Advocate Officer's Advanced Class, volunteered for Vietnam and duty with the Joint Military Team. In July 1973, after arriving at Tan Son Nhut, Scanlon was picked up by Murray and a driver in a government sedan. While riding in this car to the Joint Military Team's offices, the two Army lawyers unexpectedly found themselves under fire. Traveling in front of their vehicle was a Vietnamese Army truck full of prisoners on their way to jail at Tan Son Nhut. One of the prisoners jumped out of the truck to escape, running past the sedan carrying Scanlon and Murray. Without hesitation, a Vietnamese Army guard opened fire on the escapee with his M16 rifle. His bullets, however, missed the prisoner, striking the car carrying the lawyers. Fortunately, no one was hurt, and the escapee was recaptured. Yet, as this was his first day in country, Scanlon was sure "it would be a long year."[73]

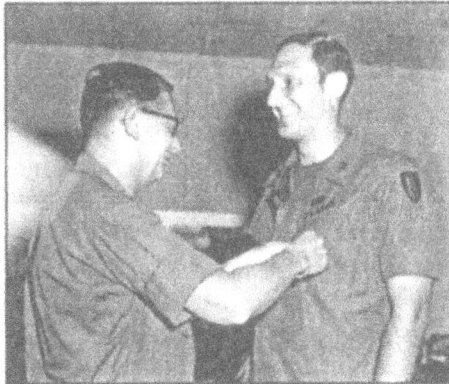

Major William K. Suter, Deputy Staff Judge Advocate, USARV, is decorated with the Bronze Star Medal by his boss, Colonel William O'Donovan, Staff Judge Advocate, USARV, at Long Binh, April 1972. Suter subsequently served as the Assistant Judge Advocate General from 1989 to 1991. He has been the Clerk of Court, U.S. Supreme Court, since retiring as a major general in 1991.

Arriving without further incident at the Joint Military Team's offices, Scanlon was assigned to the Negotiation Division. His job was to advise Col. William W. Tombaugh, the chief of the U.S. delegation, on the rights and obligations of all parties under the Paris Peace Accords. As the chief focus of the U.S. delegation was learning what happened to those personnel who had died while prisoners or who remained missing in action, this meant compiling files on missing Americans and also excavating areas under North Vietnamese and Viet Cong control in search of the remains of Americans believed buried there.

Capt. Scanlon participated in all the meetings of the Joint Military Team at which the U.S. delegation shared information on those missing in action or notified the North Vietnamese and Viet Cong of the U.S. intent to dig at likely grave sites in areas under their control. Scanlon also reviewed files on missing persons prior to the release of those papers to the North Vietnamese or Viet Cong. The United States, for example, had information from prisoners of war already released that a particular individual had been seen alive in North Vietnamese or Viet Cong custody. When the captors denied any knowledge of the missing person's location, the U.S. delegation released its evidence to them. Scanlon's task was to examine each file, ensuring not only that the information in it was accurate but also that any information disclosed was properly declassified.

During his year in South Vietnam, Scanlon journeyed by C-130 aircraft to Hanoi more than ten times. The purpose of these trips was to gain information about those Americans still missing in action. Scanlon and the other members of the U.S. delegation toured the infamous "Hanoi Hilton," where downed American pilots and aircrews had been held as prisoners of war, and made contacts with North Vietnamese government officials who might provide them with information about missing or dead Americans.

When Capt. Scanlon departed Vietnam in July 1974, he was replaced by Maj. J. Lewis Rose. Rose, who arrived in August 1974, continued providing the same legal services as had Scanlon. When Saigon fell on 30 April 1975, Rose was performing temporary duty in Hong Kong. Consequently, his tour with the Joint Military Team ended earlier than he or anyone else expected.

Summing Up

Army lawyers on duty in Vietnam between 1970 and 1975 faced challenges much different from those judge advocates who served in Southeast Asia in the early years of the conflict or during the massive buildup of the late 1960s. At MACV, Army lawyers like Col. Weaver continued their unique advisory efforts. At USARV, judge advocates like Maj. Suter wrestled with a new military justice system and a soldier population beset by drug addiction, racial strife, and mutinous behavior. In the field, military attorneys like Capt. Lamberth took to the air to ensure the delivery of legal services to front line commanders and their troops. And, as the American presence in Vietnam diminished, some judge advocates like Capts. Moushegian and Scanlon used their abilities in high-level political-military negotiations.

Almost without exception, these Army attorneys, like their predecessors in Southeast Asia, adopted new approaches in their lawyering and enhanced mission success in ways not ordinarily considered the province of judge advocates.

Notes

1. Interv, author with Brig Gen Joseph N. Tenhet, Jr., 16 Oct 96, Historians files, OTJAG.

2. Demma, "U.S. Army in Vietnam," 672-83.

3. Ibid., 687.

4. Ibid., 688.

5. Ibid., 688-89.

6. Prugh, *Law at War*, 51.

7. Ibid., 53.

8. Ibid., 59.

9. The first female judge advocate in Vietnam, Maj. Ann Wansley, served at U.S. Army, Vietnam, in 1966 and 1967. The second, Maj. Nancy A. Hunter, served at the 4th Transportation Command in 1970.

10. For statistics on U.S. Army disciplinary actions in Vietnam from 1965 to 1972, see Prugh, *Law at War*, 154.

11. Interv, author with Persons, 17 Sep 96.

12. Harold E. Parker, "Report of TJAG-Army," Judge Advocate Journal 43 (May 1971):7.

13. Kenneth J. Hodson, "Report of TJAG-Army," Judge Advocate Journal 41 (Mar 1969):7.

14. Robert D. Heinl, "The Collapse of the Armed Forces," Armed Forces Journal (7 June 1971):37.

15. Ibid., 30-31.

16. Hammond, *Military and the Media, 1968-1973*, 392.

17. Ibid., 390.

18. Prugh, *Law at War*, 107.

19. Interv, author with Col Francis A. Gilligan, 26 Jun 96, Historians files, OTJAG.

20. Interv, author with Col James O. Smyser, 24 Jun 96, Historians files, OTJAG.

21. Interv, author with Col Barry P. Steinberg, 19 Aug 96, Historians files, OTJAG.

22. MACV, Command History, 1971, II:x-9.

23. Hammond, *Military and the Media, 1968-1973*, 176, 382. See also Solis, *Marines and Military Law in Vietnam: Trial by Fire*, 129.

24. Interv, author with Steinberg, 19 Aug 96.

25. Hammond, *Military and the Media, 1968-1973*, 378-79.

26. Ibid., 385.

27. Intervs, author with Col John T. Edwards, 3 Jul 96; author with Col Leroy F. Foreman, 26 Jun 96; author with Maj Gen Kenneth D. Gray, 23 Jul 96; author with Honorable Herman F. Gierke, 26 Jun 96; author with Gilligan, 26 Jun 96; author with Tenhet, 25 Oct 96, all in Historians files, OTJAG. See also Berry, *Those Gallant Men*, 66-71; Lewy, *America in Vietnam*, 155-56.

28. William C. Westmoreland and George S. Prugh, "Judges in Command: The Judicialized Uniform Code of Military Justice in Combat," Harvard Journal of Law and Public Policy 3 (1980):4.

29. Lewy, *America in Vietnam*, 160.

30. William C. Westmoreland and George S. Prugh, "Judges in Command: The Judicialized Uniform Code of Military Justice in Combat (A Draft Code Amendment)," Harvard Journal of Law and Public Policy 4 (1981):199-201. For further commentary supporting the view that military justice failed in Vietnam, see Solis, *Marines and Military Law in Vietnam: Trial by Fire*, 241-44.

31. Report to the Judge Advocate General by the Wartime Legislation Team, Sep 83, 51, Historians files, OTJAG.

32. Ibid., 13-36.

33. Prugh, *Law at War*, 85.

34. DF, Chief, Foreign Claims Division, to USARV Staff Judge Advocate, 5 Nov 71, sub: Da Nang Ammunition Dump Cases, box 3, Records of the USARV Staff Judge Advocate, Foreign Claims, RG 472, NARA.

35. Memo, USARV Staff Judge Advocate for Deputy Commanding General USARV, 22 Jan 71, sub: Foreign Claims Operations, box 3, Records of the USARV Staff Judge Advocate Section, RG 472, NARA.

36. Ibid.; Prugh, *Law at War*, 83.

37. Memo, USARV Staff Judge Advocate for Deputy Commanding General USARV, 22 Jan 71, sub: Foreign Claims Operations.

38. DF, Chief, Foreign Claims Division, to USARV Staff Judge Advocate, 11 Oct 71, sub: Claims Against the United States Government, box 3, Records of the USARV Staff Judge Advocate Section, RG 472, NARA.

39. Summary of After Action (SAA), Staff Judge Advocate, USARV/MACV Support Command, 1973, Historians files, OTJAG.

40. Msg, Lt Gen Welborn G. Dolvin, CG, XXIV Corps, to Gen Creighton W. Abrams, COMUSMACV, 27 Aug 71, sub: US/VN Confrontations, box 3, Records of the USARV Staff Judge Advocate Section, RG 472, NARA.

41. DF, Chief, Foreign Claims Division, to USARV Staff Judge Advocate, 12 Nov 71, sub: Confrontation at HQ XXIV Corps, box 3, Records of the USARV Staff Judge Advocate Section, RG 472, NARA.

42. Interv, author with Col Donald A. Deline, 18 Sep 96, Historians files, OTJAG.

43. Ibid.

44. Ibid.

45. Hammond, *Military and the Media, 1968-1973*, 505-08. See also Keith W. Nolan, *Sappers in the Wire: The Life and Death of Firebase MARY ANN* (College Station, Tex.: Texas A&M University Press, 1995).

46. Interv, author with Maj Gen William K. Suter, 25 Jul 96, Historians files, OTJAG.

47. Ibid.

48. Interv, author with Holdaway, 24 Jul 96.

49. Ibid.

50. Ibid.

51. Interv, author with Honorable Royce C. Lamberth, 29 Jul 96, Historians files, OTJAG.

52. Ibid.

53. Ibid.

54. Interv, author with Radosh, 10 Jul 96.

55. Ltr, Maj Burnett H. Radosh to Mr & Mrs Howard R. Andrews, 23 Apr 70, Historians files, OTJAG. Only one other Army lawyer died in Vietnam. He was Lt. Col. Harold D. Krashes, who took his own life in 1971 while serving as staff judge advocate of the 23d Infantry Division.

56. Interv, author with Col Benjamin H. White, 5 Sep 96, Historians files, OTJAG.

57. Ibid.

58. Ibid.

59. Interv, author with Col Dennis M. Corrigan, 9 Jul 96, Historians files, OTJAG.

60. SAA, Staff Judge Advocate, USARV/MACV Support Command, 1973, 5.

61. Interv, author with Corrigan, 9 Jul 96.

62. Ibid.

63. SAA, Staff Judge Advocate, USARV/MACV Support Command, 1973, 7.

64. Interv, author with Corrigan, 6 Jul 96.

65. SAA, Staff Judge Advocate, USARV/MACV Support Command, 1973, 3, 5.

66. Ibid., 5.

67. Ibid., 2.

68. William E. Le Gro, *Vietnam from Cease-Fire to Capitulation* (Washington, D.C.: Government Printing Office, 1981), 18.

69. Prugh, *Law at War*, 49.

70. Interv, author with Col Vahan Moushegian, Jr., 24 Jun 96, Historians files, OTJAG.

71. Ibid.

72. Ibid.

73. Intervs, author with Lt Col Jerome W. Scanlon, 2 Aug, 28 Oct, and 30 Oct 96, Historians files, OTJAG. The rest of the section is based on these interviews.

Conclusion

This history of judge advocates in Vietnam records the experiences of a multitude of talented and dedicated soldiers. It captures their individual stories and answers the questions "Who was there?" and "What did they do?" But the narrative also demonstrates that the nature of the war in Vietnam required judge advocates to take new approaches in providing legal services and also to look at non-traditional ways to enhance mission success.

In Vietnam, the old concept that a deployed judge advocate should support the mission by delivering the same legal services offered in a peacetime garrison environment was supplanted by a new idea: that, while a judge advocate in a combat environment might still prosecute and defend at courts-martial, adjudicate claims, and provide legal assistance, an Army lawyer must take his legal practice to commanders and soldiers in the field. That same judge advocate must also look for new ways of using the law and his skills to enhance mission success. Consequently, while Army lawyers should not routinely perform nonlegal duties, the conflict in Vietnam showed that they could—and should—seek ways to use their analytical training as lawyers to recognize and solve nonlegal problems if necessary for mission accomplishment. As a result of this new idea about the role of the judge advocate in combat, an increasing number of Army lawyers assumed nontraditional roles—and addressed issues ordinarily handled by other staff principals.

From 1959 to 1962, while serving as the first judge advocates in Vietnam, Colonels Durbin and Eblen looked for ways in which the law could further the mission of their Military Assistance Advisory Group. Then Colonel Prugh, MACV staff judge advocate from 1964 to 1966, took even more far-reaching initiatives. Prugh led efforts to persuade the South Vietnamese military that its conflict with the Viet Cong and North Vietnamese was no longer an internal civil disorder. As a direct result of his work, the military—and later the government of South Vietnam—acceded to the American view that the insurgency was an armed conflict of an international character and that the benefits of the 1949 Geneva Prisoners of War Convention should be given to all captured Viet Cong and North Vietnamese soldiers. This was a public relations coup for the South Vietnamese. At the same time, applying the benefits of the Geneva Convention to those combat captives held in South Vietnam also enhanced the opportunity for survival of U.S. servicemen held by the Viet Cong and the North Vietnamese.

Colonel Prugh also reasoned that American lawyers under his authority could support U.S. military and political aims in Vietnam by helping to educate the Vietnamese about the beneficial effect of the rule of law in society. According to Prugh, "those who are familiar with the ways to combat insurgency have come to recognize that the law and lawyers have one of the most significant parts to play." That is, instilling a respect for law and order would support South Vietnam in its campaign against the terrorist activities of the Viet Cong and their North Vietnamese allies. With this goal in mind, Prugh created the Law Society of Free Vietnam. This fostered personal associations with South Vietnamese lawyers and established a forum for educating them about American legal ideas "in a manner they could accept without resentment." If the Vietnamese saw how the rule of law benefited U.S. society, they might conclude that a similar approach could improve their own legal institutions—and help counter the Communist-led insurgency.

Finally, Prugh established a unique legal advisory program that monitored the real-world operation of South Vietnam's military criminal justice system. As a result, long after George Prugh's return to the United States, MACV judge advocate advisers used their legal talents to assist the Vietnamese military on issues ranging from desertion control, resources control, and security operations to obtaining transportation for Vietnamese judge advocates, providing storage for records of trial, and obtaining materiel for local prisons.

As the war continued, Army judge advocates continued to take individual initiatives in supporting combat operations in Vietnam. At MACV headquarters, Colonel Haughney and his staff promulgated the first procedural framework for classifying combat captives, using so-called Article 5 tribunals. While the MACV provost marshal was primarily responsible for advising the Vietnamese on prisoner of war issues, judge advocates spearheaded efforts in this area—and also took the initiative in establishing a records system identifying and listing all prisoners of war. Similarly, while investigating and reporting war crimes were not judge advocate responsibilities, MACV lawyers took the lead in formulating guidance on investigating and reporting such crimes. By 1968 the Military Assistance Command, Vietnam, had decided, as a matter of policy, that judge advocates would be the primary focal point for all war crimes issues.

Judge advocates also enhanced mission success by providing legal support to decision makers outside the Army and the Department of Defense. Like his predecessors, Colonels Prugh and Haughney,

Colonel Williams, MACV staff judge advocate from August 1969 to July 1970, provided legal advice to the U.S. ambassador and his staff. As the senior government lawyer in Vietnam, it was only natural for the MACV staff judge advocate to respond directly to inquiries from the top State Department officer in the country. In addition to meeting at least weekly with the U.S. ambassador, however, Colonel Williams expanded his role as an adviser and counselor while a member of the Irregular Practices Committee. This committee was composed of civilian representatives of the U.S. Overseas Mission and officers from MACV staff sections, including Colonel Williams as the MACV staff judge advocate. While officially tasked with coordinating the suppression of black-marketing, currency manipulation, and other illegal activities affecting the Vietnamese economy, the committee's composition naturally made it a clearinghouse for a variety of policy issues—and a point of contact for Saigon government officials seeking assistance. As a result, by the time he departed Vietnam in 1970 Colonel Williams was conferring weekly with the Vietnamese minister of finance, the director of customs, the minister of economy, and representatives of the U.S. Agency for International Development and the U.S. embassy.

Meanwhile, Army lawyers outside Saigon used their individual talents and abilities in a variety of nontraditional ways. At USARV headquarters in Long Binh, for example, after General McCaffrey demanded that "something" be done about soldier drug addicts, Major Suter spearheaded the creation of a Drug Abuser Holding Center. There, "all second time drug abusers" from any subordinate USARV unit were held until they could be administratively eliminated from the Army and medically evaluated for treatment in the United States. This was a novel and efficient method for handling soldiers whose drug addiction made treatment more appropriate than punishment by courts-martial.

Army lawyers at brigades and divisions in the field took similar initiatives. At the 5,000-man 173d Airborne Brigade, for example, Captain White volunteered to work as an operations officer in addition to his judge advocate duties. Further, after General Williams, the commander, lost confidence in the ability of his brigade adjutant to process awards and decorations properly, Captain White and the brigade's other judge advocate assumed these G1 duties. Another example of an Army lawyer enhancing mission success in new ways was Colonel Holdaway's innovative approach to practicing law in the Army's new airmobile experiment, the 1st Cavalry Division. With about 450 helicopters, the division had a very large area of operations, and this meant that Holdaway and his lawyers had to take their legal services to the field. As a result, the division's military attorneys were often airborne, flying out to basecamps and firebases on the "lawbird" to confer with and advise commanders—as well as provide personal legal assistance to their soldiers.

Finally, after the signing of the Paris Peace Accords, judge advocates serving on the Four Party Joint Military Commission and Four Party Joint Military Team between 1973 and 1975 did more than traditional lawyering. Thus, Captain Moushegian served as the U.S. delegation's expert on the peace treaty's provisions and also assumed the duties of principal liaison officer—meeting regularly with his Viet Cong, South Vietnamese, and North Vietnamese counterparts in what was essentially a diplomatic role. Similarly, Captain Scanlon, one of the last Army lawyers to serve in Vietnam, advised the chief of the U.S. delegation on the rights and obligations of all parties under the Paris Peace Accords. But Scanlon also assisted in gathering information on Americans still missing in action—which meant traveling to Hanoi, touring the infamous "Hanoi Hilton," and making contact with North Vietnamese government officials who might provide information about missing or dead Americans.

What was the reason for this significant number of individual initiatives? Certainly the nature of the Vietnam War itself encouraged nontraditional approaches to mission accomplishment. The unconventional nature of the guerrilla insurgency required responses that were novel, if not radical. The Army experimented with an airmobile division and created new combat units—Special Forces—adept at both combat and "winning hearts and minds." Seen from this perspective, efforts such as Prugh's advisory program were a perfect complement to initiatives in the Army generally.

Another reason for increased individual initiative, however, certainly resulted from the reality that there were more lawyers in the Army than ever before. During World War II, for example, an armored division of 11,000 soldiers was authorized one judge advocate on its Table of Manpower. As other divisions were similarly structured, judge advocates participating in the fighting in Europe or the Pacific had little time for issues outside the established areas of military justice, claims, legal assistance, and administrative law. But, as the Judge Advocate General's Corps increased in size during the Vietnam buildup—-an expansion that accelerated after more lawyers were needed to satisfy the new requirements of the Military Justice Act of

1968—-there simply were more judge advocates in the corps. Many were not content to adhere to the old concept of the traditional role of lawyers in uniform. Better-educated, exceptionally energetic, and unfettered by old approaches to lawyering, these judge advocates looked for new ways to serve.

By the time the war ended in Vietnam, an increasing number of judge advocates had taken individual initiatives to enhance mission success in ways not ordinarily considered to be part of normal judge advocate duties. As future events would show, the role of the judge advocate would change as a result of the Army's experiences in Vietnam. It would no longer be enough for Army lawyers deployed in military operations to support their units in the same manner as judge advocates would support a commander and staff at a U.S. Army installation during peacetime. On the contrary, the My Lai massacre and the resulting Department of Defense creation of a Law of War program—and a subsequent and complementary Joint Chiefs of Staff directive requiring the chairman's legal counsel to review all operations plans—required the Army's legal corps to take primary responsibility for ensuring that "the Armed Forces of the United States shall comply with the law of war in the conduct of military operations and related activities in armed conflict."

A few perceptive Army lawyers realized that this meant judge advocates must review all operations plans, concept plans, rules of engagement, execution orders, deployment orders, policies, and directives to ensure compliance with the Law of War, as well as with domestic and international law. These same military lawyers also recognized that this could best be accomplished if judge advocates were integrated into operations at all levels, and while Army lawyers were not routinely to perform nonlegal duties, effective integration would sometimes require judge advocates to take on nonlegal tasks.

That story—the increasing integration of judge advocates into Army operations in the 1980s and 1990s—is not part of this history. That said, the subsequent development of operational law as a legal discipline and the emergence of a new role for uniformed lawyers in the Army owe much to the trail blazing done by those who served in Southeast Asia from 1959 to 1975. If nothing else, these soldier-lawyers showed the way for those who followed them.

Bibliography

The location of various unpublished sources is indicated by the following abbreviations:

ACMR Army Court of Military Review

NARA National Archives and Records Administration, College Park, Maryland, and St. Louis, Missouri

OTJAG Office of the Judge Advocate General, Washington, D.C.

TJAGSA The Judge Advocate General's School, U.S. Army, Charlottesville, Virginia

USALSA U.S. Army Legal Services Agency, Arlington, Virginia

Primary Sources

Official Records

Agreement on Ending the War and Restoring Peace in Viet-Nam [Paris Peace Accords]. 27 January 1973. Published in U.S. Treaties and Other International Acts Series 24 (1973), page 1.

Annual Report of the United States Court of Military Appeals and The Judge Advocates General of the Armed Forces and the General Counsel of the Department of the Treasury Pursuant to the Uniform Code of Military Justice, 1952–66. Washington, D.C.: Government Printing Office, 1954–67.

Annual Report of the U.S. Court of Military Appeals and The Judge Advocates General of the Armed Forces and the General Counsel of the Department of Transportation Pursuant to the Uniform Code of Military Justice, 1967–83. Washington, D.C.: Government Printing Office, 1968–83.

Foreign Claims Act. Title 10, United States Code, Section 2734.

Geneva Convention for Amelioration of the Condition of the Wounded and Sick in Armed Forces in the Field. 12 August 1949. Published in U.S. Treaties and Other International Acts Series no. 3326 and in DA Pamphlet 27–1, *Treaties Governing Land Warfare* (Washington, D.C.: Department of the Army, 1956).

Geneva Convention Relative to the Protection of Civilian Persons in Time of War. 12 August 1949. Published in U.S. Treaties and Other International

Acts Series 3356 and in DA Pamphlet 27–1, *Treaties Governing Land Warfare* (Washington, D.C.: Department of the Army, 1956).

Geneva Convention Relative to the Treatment of Prisoners of War. 12 August 1949. Published in U.S. Treaties and Other International Acts Series 3364 and in DA Pamphlet 27–1, *Treaties Governing Land Warfare* (Washington, D.C.: Department of the Army, 1956).

Hague Convention No. IV Respecting the Laws and Customs of War on Land and Annex Thereto Embodying Regulations Respecting the Laws and Customs of War on Land. 18 October 1907. U.S. Statutes 36: 2277, reprinted in DA Pamphlet 27–1, *Treaties Governing Land Warfare* (Washington, D.C.: Department of the Army, 1956).

Judge Advocate General, U.S. Army, Office of the. *JAGC Personnel and Activity Directory*. Washington, D.C.: Office of the Judge Advocate General, 1962–75.

————. Report to the Judge Advocate General by the Wartime Legislation Team. September 1983. TJAGSA.

Military Assistance Advisory Group (MAAG), Vietnam, Headquarters. MAAG Vietnam Judge Advocate Responsibilities, Appendix I to Annex L (Legal), MAAG Vietnam OPLAN 61–61. 10 February 1961. Record Group (RG) 334, NARA.

————. Memorandum no. 10, Missions and Functions of MAAG Advisers. 27 January 1961. RG 334, NARA.

Military Assistance Command, Vietnam (MACV), Headquarters. Memorandum, sub: Resources Control—Arrest, Search, and Seizure Laws in the Republic of Vietnam. 21 January 1965. Historians files, OTJAG.

————. Memorandum, sub: RVNAF [Republic of Vietnam Armed Forces] Military Justice. 12 February 1965. Historians files, OTJAG.

————. Memorandum, sub: Summary and Outline of RVN Judicial and Police Functions. 24 February 1965. Historians files, OTJAG.

————. Memorandum for Record, sub: Status of Forces in Thailand. 17 July 1962. Historians files, OTJAG.

————. Staff Study, "Purpose: To examine the role of the Civil Law in counterinsurgency in Vietnam and to make pertinent recommendations." 31 May 1965. Historians files, OTJAG.

Military Justice Act of 1968. Public Law no. 90–632, U.S. Statutes at Large 82: 1335.

Mutual Defense Assistance in Indochina [Pentalateral Agreement]. 23 December 1950. Reprinted in Prugh, *Law at War*, Appendix I.

1977 Protocols Additional to the Geneva Conventions. 12 December 1977. Published in International Legal Materials 16: 1391 and in Department of the Army Pamphlet 27–1–1, *Protocols to the Geneva Conventions of 12 August 1949* (Washington, D.C.: Department of the Army, 1979).

U.S. Army. *Report of the Investigation (Volume I), Report to the Department of the Army, Review of the Preliminary Investigation into the My Lai Incident [Peers Report]*. 14 March 1970. Reprinted in Joseph Goldstein, Burke Marshall, and Jack Schwartz. *The My Lai Massacre and Its Cover-up: Beyond the Reach of the Law?* (New York: Free Press, 1976).

Vienna Convention on Diplomatic Relations. 18 April 1961. Published in United States Treaties 3: 3227 and in International Legal Materials 8: 679 (1969).

Directives, Instructions, Manuals, Pamphlets, and Regulations

AR 27–52, *Consular Protection of Foreign Nationals Subject to the Uniform Code of Military Justice*. 5 November 1968.

AR 350–216, *Training: The Geneva Conventions of 1949 and Hague Convention No. IV of 1907*. 28 May 1970.

AR 500–50, *Civil Disturbances*. 1 June 1972.

AR 608–4, *Control and Registration of War Trophies and War Trophy Firearms*. 28 August 1969.

AR 635–200, *Personnel Separations, Enlisted Personnel*. 15 July 1966.

AR 700–99, *Acquisition, Accounting, Control, and Disposal of Captured Enemy Equipment and Foreign Material*. 15 July 1976.

AR 755–2, *Disposal of Excess, Surplus, Foreign Excess, Captured, and Unwanted Materiel*. 24 July 1970.

Department of the Army (DA) Field Manual (FM) 19–40, *Enemy Prisoners of War, Civilian Internees and Detained Persons*. February 1976.

FM 27–10, *The Law of Land Warfare*. 1956.

Department of the Army Pamphlet (DA Pam) 27–1, *Treaties Governing Land Warfare*. December 1956.

DA Pam 27–1–1, *Protocols to the Geneva Conventions of 12 August 1949*. September 1979.

DA Pam 27–24, *Selected International Agreements*, Vol. II. December 1976.

DA Pam 27–161–1, *Law of Peace*, Vol. I. September 1979.

DA Pam 27–161–2, *International Law*, Vol. II. October 1962.

124

Department of the Army. Office of the Chief of Staff. Chief of Staff Regulation 11–2, *Army Programs: Implementation of DoD Law of War Program.* 7 May 1975.

Department of Defense (DoD). DoD Directive 2000.11, *Procedures for Handling Requests for Political Asylum and Temporary Refuge.* 3 March 1972.

DoD Directive 5100.69, *DoD Enemy PW/Detainee Program.* 27 December 1972.

DoD Directive 5100.77, *DoD Program for the Implementation of the Law of War.* 5 November 1974, 10 July 1979.

Manual for Courts-Martial, U.S. Army, 1928, A. Washington, D.C.: Government Printing Office, 1927.

Manual for Courts-Martial, United States, 1949. Washington, D.C.: Government Printing Office, 1948.

Manual for Courts-Martial, United States, 1951. Washington, D.C.: Government Printing Office, 1951.

Manual for Courts-Martial, United States, 1969. Washington, D.C.: Government Printing Office, 1969.

Military Assistance Command, Vietnam (MACV). MACV Directive 20–4, *Inspections and Investigations of War Crimes.* 18 May 1968. Reprinted in Prugh, *Law at War*, Appendix F.

MACV Directive 20–5, *Inspections and Investigations: Prisoners of War—Determination of Eligibility.* 17 May 1966, 21 September 1966.

MACV Directive 25–1, *Claims.* 14 May 1965.

MACV Directive 27–1, *Litigation: Legal Services and Litigation.* 16 April 1965.

MACV Directive 27–4, *Legal Services: Foreign Jurisdiction Procedures and Information.* 2 November 1967.

MACV Directive 27–5, *Legal Services: War Crimes, and Other Prohibited Acts.* 2 November 1967.

MACV Directive 27–6, *Legal Services and Legal Obligations in Vietnam.* 16 June 1965, 14 September 1968.

MACV Directive 190–3, *Military Police: Enemy Prisoners of War.* 6 April 1967.

MACV Directive 335–1, *Reports of Serious Crimes or Other Incidents.* 5 January 1966.

MACV Directive 381–46, *Military Intelligence: Combined Screening of Detainees*. 27 December 1967.

U.S. Army, Vietnam. Supplement 1 to AR 27–10, *Military Justice*. 15 June 1970.

Cases

Morrison v. *United States*, F. Supp. 316 (1970): 78.

United States v. *Calley*, Court Martial (CM) 426402, Court-Martial Reports (CMR) 46: 1131 (ACMR 1973), affirmed CMR 48: 19 (U.S. Court of Military Appeals [CMA]); see also *Calley* v. *Calloway*, F. Supp. 382 (1974): 650, *Calley* v. *Hoffmann*, F. 2d 519 (1975): 814, certiorari (cert.) denied, U.S. 425 (1976): 911.

United States v. Duffy, CM 424795, CMR 47: 658 (ACMR 1973).

United States v. C. Garcia, CM 416159, CMR 38: 625 (Army Board of Military Review [ABMR] 1967).

United States v. J. Garcia, CM 416160 (1967). USALSA.

United States v. Gervase, CM 416161 (1967). USALSA.

United States v. Goldman, CM 420332, CMR 43: 77 (ACMR 1970).

United States v. Griffen, CMR 39: 586 (ABMR 1968).

United States v. Henderson, CM 428589 (1972). USALSA.

United States v. Hodges, CM 420341 (1969). USALSA.

United States v. Levy, CM 416463, CMR 39: 672 (ABMR 1968); Levy v. Resor, 37 CMR 399 (CMA 1968).

United States v. Lund, United States v. Francis, CM 420181 (1969). USALSA.

United States v. McGee, CM 422412 (1969). USALSA.

United States v. Medina, CM 427162 (1971). USALSA.

United States v. Rowland, CM 421750 (1969). USALSA.

United States v. Thomas, CM 416162, CMR 38: 655 (ABMR 1968).

United States v. Williams, CM 419872 (1968). USALSA.

United States v. Woods, CM 416803 (1966). USALSA.

Interviews

The author conducted interviews with the following individuals:

Brig. Gen. Bruce C. Babbitt, Mr. J. Stevens Berry, Col. John R. Bozeman, Mr. Samuel T. Brick, Jr., Col. Fred Bright, Jr., Col. Raymond D. Cole, Col.

Dennis M. Corrigan, Col. Jack H. Crouchet, Lt. Col. Leonard G. Crowley, Brig. Gen. Thomas R. Cuthbert, Col. Donald A. Deline, Col. Dean R. Dort, Col. John J. Douglass, Col. Joseph Dudzik, Col. Paul J. Durbin, Lt. Col. George C. Eblen, Col. William G. Eckhardt, Col. John T. Edwards, Col. Ned E. Felder, Col. Leroy F. Foreman, Hon. Herman F. Gierke, Col. Francis A. Gilligan, Maj. Gen. Kenneth D. Gray, Col. Fred K. Green, Brig. Gen. Donald W. Hansen, Col. Edward W. Haughney, Brig. Gen. Ronald M. Holdaway, Col. Dennis R. Hunt, Col. Robert H. Ivey, Mr. Robert N. Kittel, Hon. Royce C. Lamberth, Col. Alfred E. McNamee, Col. Vahan Moushegian, Lt. Col. William G. Myers, Col. Hubert E. Miller, Maj. Gen. Wilton B. Persons, Maj. Gen. George S. Prugh, Col. Burnett H. Radosh, Col. Raymond C. Ruppert, Lt. Col. Jerome W. Scanlon, Col. James R. Smith, Col. James O. Smyser, Col. Barry P. Steinberg, Maj. Gen. William K. Suter, Col. Arthur H. Taylor, Brig. Gen. Joseph N. Tenhet, Col. Benjamin H. White, Col. Charles A. White, Maj. Gen. Lawrence H. Williams.

Military Personnel Records, National Personnel Records Center, NARA

The author consulted the personnel records of the following individuals:

Brig. Gen. Bruce C. Babbitt, Col. Fred Bright, Jr., Col. Raymond D. Cole, Lt. Col. Leonard G. Crowley, Col. Dean R. Dort, Col. John J. Douglass, Col. Paul J. Durbin, Col. Ned E. Felder, Lt. Col. George C. Eblen, Col. Leroy F. Foreman, Col. Francis A. Gilligan, Col. Herbert J. Green, Lt. Col. Guy A. Hamlin, Col. Edward W. Haughney, Brig. Gen. Ronald M. Holdaway, Col. Irvin M. Kent, Lt. Col. John N. Kulish, Col. Alfred A. McNamee, Maj. Ralph G. Miranda, Lt. Col. William G. Myers, Col. George R. Robinson, Lt. Col. Jerome W. Scanlon, Jr., Col. John T. Sherwood, Jr., Col. Arthur H. Taylor, Brig. Gen. Joseph N. Tenhet, Jr., Col. Robert K. Weaver, Lt. Col. John P. Weber, Col. George F. Westerman, Col. Charles A. White, Jr.

Secondary Sources

Books

Anderson, David L., ed. *Facing My Lai: Moving Beyond the Massacre.* Lawrence, Kans.: University Press of Kansas, 1998.

Berry, J. Stevens. *Those Gallant Men.* Novato, Calif.: Presidio Press, 1984.

Bilton, Michael, and Kevin Sim. *Four Hours in My Lai.* New York: Viking Press, 1972.

Borch, Frederic L. *Judge Advocates in Combat: Army Lawyers in Military Operations from Vietnam to Haiti.* Washington, D.C.: U.S. Army Center of Military History, 2001.

Burkett, B. G., and Glenna Whitley. *Stolen Valor*. Dallas, Tex.: Verity Press, 1998.

Clarke, Jeffrey J. *Advice and Support: The Final Years, 1965–1973. U.S. Army in Vietnam*. Washington, D.C.: U.S. Army Center of Military History, 1987.

Crouchet, Jack H. *Vietnam Stories: A Judge's Memoir*. Niwot, Colo.: University Press of Colorado, 1997.

Donovan, David. *Once a Warrior King*. New York: McGraw-Hill, 1985.

Dorland, Gil. *Legacy of Discord*. Washington, D.C.: Brassey's, 2001.

Eckhardt, George S. *Command and Control, 1950–1969*. Vietnam Studies. Washington, D.C.: Department of the Army, 1974.

Generous, William T., Jr. *Swords and Scales: The Development of the Uniform Code of Military Justice*. New York: Kennikat Press, 1973.

Griffith, Robert K., Jr. *The U.S. Army's Transition to the All-Volunteer Force, 1968–1974*. Washington, D.C.: U.S. Army Center of Military History, 1997.

Hammond, William H. *Public Affairs: The Military and the Media, 1962–1968*. U.S. Army in Vietnam. Washington, D.C.: U.S. Army Center of Military History, 1988.

———. *Public Affairs: The Military and the Media, 1968–1973*. U.S. Army in Vietnam. Washington, D.C.: U.S. Army Center of Military History, 1996.

Hersh, Seymour. *My Lai 4: A Report on the Massacre and Its Aftermath*. New York: Random House, 1970.

House, Jonathan M. *The United States Army in Joint Operations, 1950–1983*. Washington, D.C.: U.S. Army Center of Military History, 1992.

Judge Advocate General's Corps, U.S. Army. *The Army Lawyer: A History of the Judge Advocate General's Corps, 1775–1975*. Washington, D.C.: Government Printing Office, 1975.

Karnow, Stanley. *Vietnam: A History*. New York: Viking Press, 1983.

Krepinevich, Andrew F. *The Army and Vietnam*. Baltimore: Johns Hopkins University Press, 1986.

Lang, Daniel. *Casualties of War*. New York: McGraw, 1969.

Le Gro, William E. *Vietnam from Cease-Fire to Capitulation*. Washington, D.C.: Government Printing Office, 1981.

Lewy, Guenter. *America in Vietnam*. New York: Oxford University Press, 1978.

Lurie, Jonathan. *Pursuing Military Justice*. Princeton, N.J.: Princeton University Press, 1998.

McDonough, James. *Platoon Leader*. Novato, Calif.: Presidio Press, 1985.

MacGarrigle, George L. *Taking the Offensive, October 1966 to October 1967*. U.S. Army in Vietnam. Washington, D.C.: U.S. Army Center of Military History, 1998.

McMaster, H. R. *Dereliction of Duty*. New York: HarperCollins Publishers, 1997.

Meyer, Harold J. *Hanging Sam: A Military Biography of General Samuel T. Williams*. Denton, Tex.: University of North Texas Press, 1990.

Meyerson, Joel D. *Images of a Lengthy War*. U.S. Army in Vietnam. Washington, D.C.: U.S. Army Center of Military History, 1989.

Moore, Harold G., and Joseph L. Galloway. *We Were Soldiers Once, and Young: The Battle of the Ia Drang Valley*. New York: Random House, 1992.

Natkiel, Richard. *Atlas of American Wars*. Greenwich, Conn.: Bison Books, 1986.

Nolan, William K. *Sappers in the Wire: The Life and Death of Firebase Maryann*. College Park: Texas A&M Press, 1995.

Olson, James S., and Randy Roberts. *My Lai: A Brief History with Documents*. New York: St. Martin's Press, 1998.

———. *The 25-Year War: America's Military Role in Vietnam*. Lexington: University Press of Kentucky, 1984.

Peers, William R. *The My Lai Inquiry*. New York: Norton, 1979.

Prugh, George S. *Law at War: Vietnam, 1964–1973*. Vietnam Studies. Washington, D.C.: Department of the Army, 1975.

Sheehan, Neil. *A Bright Shining Lie*. New York: Random House, 1988.

Reisman, W. Michael, and Chris T. Antoniou. *The Laws of War*. New York: Vintage Books, 1994.

Sherrill, Robert. *Military Justice Is to Justice as Military Music Is to Music*. New York: Harper and Row, 1970.

Solis, Gary D. *Marines and Military Law: Trial by Fire*. Washington, D.C.: Marine Corps History and Museums Division, 1989.

————. *Son Thang: An American War Crime*. Annapolis, Md.: Naval Institute Press, 1997.

Sorley, Lewis. *Thunderbolt: General Creighton Abrams and the Army of His Times*. New York: Simon and Schuster, 1992.

Spector, Ronald H. *Advice and Support: The Early Years, 1941–1960*. U.S. Army in Vietnam. Washington, D.C.: U.S. Army Center of Military History, 1983.

Stanton, Shelby. *The Rise and Fall of an American Army: U.S. Ground Forces in Vietnam, 1965–1973*. Novato, Calif.: Presidio Press, 1985.

Stein, Jeff. *A Murder in Wartime*. New York: St. Martin's Press, 1992.

Summers, Harry G., Jr. *Historical Atlas of the Vietnam War*. Boston: Houghton Mifflin, 1995.

————. *On Strategy: A Critical Analysis of the Vietnam War*. Novato, Calif.: Presidio Press, 1982.

Taylor, Telford. *Nuremburg and Vietnam: An American Tragedy*. Chicago: Quadrangle Books, 1970.

Vien, Cao Van. *The Final Collapse*. Indochina Monographs. Washington, D.C.: Government Printing Office, 1983.

Whitlow, Robert H. *U.S. Marines in Vietnam, 1954–1964*. Washington, D.C.: Headquarters, U.S. Marine Corps, 1977.

Wiener, Frederick B. *Civilians Under Military Justice*. Chicago: University of Chicago Press, 1967.

Winthrop, William. *Military Law and Precedents*. 2d ed. Washington, D.C.: Government Printing Office, 1920.

Articles

Addicott, Jeffrey F., and William A. Hudson, Jr. "The Twenty-fifth Anniversary of My Lai: A Time to Inculcate the Lessons." *Military Law Review* 139 (Winter 1993): 153–85.

Barn, Thomas. "Fragging: A Study." *ARMY* (April 1977): 46.

Bond, Thomas C. "Fragging: A Study." *American Journal of Psychiatry* 133 (1976): 1328–31.

Borch, Frederic L. "Bolsheviks, Polar Bears, and Military Law: The Experiences of Army Lawyers in North Russia and Siberia in World War I." *Prologue* 30 (Fall 1998): 180–91.

————. "Law of War Training: A Practical Program." *Infantry* (November–December 1985): 33.

Borek, Ted. "Legal Services During War." *Military Law Review* 120 (Spring 1988): 1.

Burger, James A. "International Law—The Role of the Legal Adviser, and Law of War Instruction." *Army Lawyer* (September 1978): 22.

Currier, Roger M., and Irvin M. Kent. "The Boards of Review of the Armed Services." *Vanderbilt Law Review* 6 (February 1953): 241–50.

Damarest, Geoffrey. "Updating the Geneva Conventions: The 1977 Protocols." *Army Lawyer* (November 1983): 18.

Demma, Vincent. "The U.S. Army in Vietnam." In *American Military History, rev. ed. Washington, D.C.: U.S. Army Center of Military History, 1989.*

Denny, Michael C. "The Impact of Article 82 of Protocol I to the 1949 Geneva Conventions on the Organization and Operation of a Division SJA Office." *Army Lawyer* (April 1980): 14.

Douglass, John J. "The Judicialization of Military Courts." *Hastings Law Journal* 22 (January 1971): 213–35.

Eckhardt, William. "Command Criminal Responsibility." *Military Law Review* 97 (Summer 1982): 1–34.

Ervin, Sam J., Jr. "The Military Justice Act of 1968." *Military Law Review* 45 (July 1969): 77–98.

———. "The Military Justice Act of 1968." *Wake Forest Law Review* 5 (1969): 223.

Fratcher, William F. "History of The Judge Advocate General's Corps, United States Army." *Military Law Review* 4 (March 1959): 89–122.

Green, Fred K. "The Cease-Fire." In *Report of the Sixth International Congress of the International Society of Military Criminal Law and the Law of War I* (May 1973): 199–249.

———. "The Concept of War and the Concept of Combatant in Modern Conflicts." *Military Law and Law of War Review* (1971): 267–309.

Heinl, Robert D., Jr. "The Collapse of the Armed Forces." *Armed Forces Journal* (7 June 1971): 31.

Hodson, Kenneth J. "The Manual for Courts-Martial—1969." *Military Law Review* 57 (Summer 1972): 1–16.

———. "The Military Justice Act." *Judge Advocate Journal*, Bulletin no. 42 (May 1970): 30–38.

———. "Report of TJAG—Army." *Judge Adovcate Journal*, Bulletin no. 38 (December 1966): 9–11.

————. "Report of TJAG—Army." *Judge Advocate Journal*, Bulletin no. 41 (March 1969): 7.

————. "Report of TJAG—Army." *Judge Advocate Journal*, Bulletin no. 42 (May 1970): 4–7.

Hunt, Dennis R. "Viet Nam Hustings." *Judge Advocate Journal*, Bulletin no. 44 (July 1972): 23.

Kent, Irvin M., Jon N. Kulish, Ned E. Felder, and Herbert Green. "A Lawyer's Day in Vietnam." *American Bar Association Journal* 54 (December 1968): 1177.

King, Archibald. "Changes in the Uniform Code of Justice Necessary To Make It Workable in Time of War." *Federal Bar Journal* 22 (Winter 1962): 49–59.

Kuhfeld, Albert M. "Amendments to Article 15, Uniform Code of Military Justice." *Judge Advocate Journal Bulletin* 34 (1963): 69–80.

Levie, Howard S. "Compliance by States with the 1949 Geneva Prisoner of War Convention." *Army Lawyer* (June 1974): 1.

Linden, Eugene. "Fragging and Other Withdrawal Symptoms." *Saturday Review* (8 January 1972): 12.

Matthews, Ann. "Army JAG's Search for Justice." *Vietnam* (December 1998): 30–36.

Morgan, Edmund M. "The Background of the Uniform Code of Military Justice." *Vanderbilt Law Review* 6 (1953): 169–85.

————. "The Existing Court-Martial System and the Ansell Articles." *Yale Law Journal* 29 (November 1919): 52–74.

Nardotti, Michael J., Jr. "General Ken Hodson—A Thoroughly Remarkable Man." *Military Law Review* 151 (Winter 1996): 202–15.

Norsworthy, Levator, Jr. "Organization for Battle: The Judge Advocate's Responsibility Under Article 82 of Protocol I to the Geneva Conventions." *Military Law Review* 93 (Summer 1981): 9–24.

Parker, Harold E. "Report of TJAG—Army." *Judge Advocate Journal* 43 (May 1971): 7.

Parks, Hays W. "A Few Tools in the Prosecution of War Crimes." *Military Law Review* 149 (Summer 1995): 73–85.

————. "Command Responsibility for War Crimes." *Military Law Review* 62 (Fall 1973): 1–104.

Prugh, George S. "The Code of Conduct for the Armed Forces." *Columbia Law Review* 56 (May 1956): 678.

————. "Denims, Pinks and Greens." Manuscript, January 1994. Historians files, OTJAG.

————. "Introduction to William Winthrop's 'Military Law and Precedents.'" *Military Law and Law of War Review 27 (1988): 437–70.*

————. "Law Practice in the Vietnam War." *Federal Bar Journal* 27 (Winter 1967): 57.

Scanlon, Jerome W. "SJA Spotlight: U.S. Delegation, Four-Party Joint Military Team." *Army Lawyer* (March 1974): 14.

Schlueter, David. "The Court-Martial: A Historical Survey." *Military Law Review* 87 (Winter 1980): 129.

Walker, Daniel, and C. George Niebank. "The Court of Military Appeals—Its History, Organization and Operation." *Vanderbilt Law Review* 6 (February 1953): 228–40.

Ward, Chester. "The UCMJ—Does It Work?" *Vanderbilt Law Review* 6 (February 1953): 186–227.

Webb, James H. "The Sad Conviction of Sam Green: The Case for the Reasonable and Honest War Criminal." *Res Ipsa Loquitur; Georgetown Review of Law and Public Interest* 26 (Winter 1974): 11.

Westerman, George F. "A New Approach in Disseminating the Geneva Conventions." *Military Law Review* 45 (July 1969): 99–105.

————. "Military Justice in the Republic of Vietnam." *Military Law Review* 31 (January 1966): 137–58.

Westmoreland, William C., and George S. Prugh. "Judges in Command: The Judicialized Uniform Code of Military Justice in Combat." *Harvard Journal of Law and Public Policy* 4 (1980): 1.

Wiener, Frederick B. "Courts-Martial and the Bill of Rights: the Original Practice." *Military Law Review* Bicentennial Issue (1975): 171.

————. "Courts-Martial for Civilians Accompanying the Armed Forces in Vietnam." *American Bar Association Journal* 54 (January 1968): 24.

————. "Martial Law Today." *American Bar Association Journal* 55 (August 1969): 723.

————. "The Perils of Tinkering with Military Justice." *ARMY (November 1970): 8–12.*

Willis, John T. "The United States Court of Military Appeals: Its Origin, Operation and Future." *Military Law Review* 55 (Winter 1972): 39–93.

Wilson, William. "I Had Prayed to God . . ." *American Heritage: Battles and Leaders* (1994): 54–63.

Biographical Notes on Army Lawyers

While more than one hundred judge advocates are mentioned by name in this work, there are only about forty biographical sketches in this appendix. As a general rule, the decision to include information on a particular individual was based on whether that person's experiences in Vietnam were examined in the narrative; judge advocates mentioned in passing are not included.

Official personnel records maintained by the National Personnel Records Center, St. Louis, Missouri, along with data cards and personnel directories on file at the Personnel, Plans, and Training Office, Office of the Judge Advocate General, were the principal sources for biographical information on retired or deceased judge advocates. Department of the Army Officer Record Briefs provided the biographical data for judge advocates in the Army's active and reserve components. While all information is believed to be accurate, any errors of commission or omission are the responsibility of the author.

Abbreviations:

Abn	Airborne
ACC	Army Court of Criminal Appeals
ACMR	Army Court of Military Review
ACR	Armored Cavalry Regiment
Adm	Administrative
Adv	Adviser
AFB	Air Force Base
Affrs	Affairs
AJAG	Assistant Judge Advocate General
Arm	Armor
Armd	Armored
Arty	Artillery
Asslt	Assault
Asst	Assistant
Atty	Attorney
Aug	Augmentation
BA/S	Bachelor of Art/Science
Bde	Brigade
Br	Branch
Brks	Barracks

CAC	Combined Arms Center, Fort Leavenworth, KS
CAD	Contract Appeals Division
Cav	Cavalry
C&GSC	Command and General Staff College, Fort Leavenworth, KS
Cdr	Commander
Ch	Chief
Civ	Civil
CJA	Command Judge Advocate
CJCS	Chairman of the Joint Chiefs of Staff, Washington, D.C.
Cmd	Command
Cmdt	Commandant
Commd	Commissioned
Commr	Commissioner
Cnsl	Counsel
Coll	College
CONUS	Continental United States
Ctr	Center
DA	Department of the Army
DAD	Defense Appellate Division, Falls Church, VA
DC	Defense Counsel
Def	Defense
Dep	Deputy
Det	Detachment
Div	Division
DoD	Department of Defense
Dscpl	Disciplinary
Eng	Engineer
Enl	Enlisted
Exec	Executive
FECOM	Far East Command
FORSCOM	U.S. Forces Command, Fort McPherson, GA
Ft	Fort
GAD	Government Appellate Division, Falls Church, VA
Grp	Group
IG	Inspector General
IMA	Individual Mobilization Augmentee
INSCOM	Intelligence and Security Command
Instr	Instructor

Intl	International
JA	Judge Advocate
JAGC/D	Judge Advocate General's Corps/Department
JAGO	Judge Advocate General's Office, Washington, D.C.
JCS	Joint Chiefs of Staff
JD	Juris Doctor
JFKSWC	J. F. Kennedy Special Warfare Center, Fort Bragg, NC
JTF	Joint Task Force
Jus	Justice
Lgl	Legal
Lit	Litigation
LLB/M	Bachelor of Laws/Master of Laws
Log	Logistical
LSO	Legal Services Organization
MAAG	Military Assistance Advisory Group
MACV	Military Assistance Command, Vietnam
M Ed	Master of Education
Med	Medical
MEDCOM	Medical Command
MDW	Military District of Washington, Washington, D.C.
Mil	Military
MJ	Military Judge
MA/S	Master of Arts/Science
Mgmt	Management
MP	Military Police
MPA	Masters of Public Administration
MTMC	Military Traffic Management Command
Natl	National
NG	National Guard
Ofc	Office
Off	Officer
OGC	Office of the General Counsel
OIC	Officer in Charge
OJA	Office of the Judge Advocate, U.S. Army, Europe
Opnl	Operational
Opns	Operations
Org	Organization
OTJAG	Office of the Judge Advocate General, Washington, D.C.

OSJA	Office of the Staff Judge Advocate
Pers	Personnel
PP&TO	Personnel, Plans, and Training Office, OTJAG
Rcrtg	Recruiting
RDC	Regional Defense Counsel
REFRAD	Released from active duty
Regt	Regiment
Retd	Retired
Sch	School
Scty	Security
Svc	Service
SDC	Senior Defense Counsel
SF	Special Forces
S&F	Staff and Faculty
SJA	Staff Judge Advocate
Sp	Special
Spt	Support
St	State
Strat	Strategic
SUPCOM	Support Command
TAACOM	Theater Army Area Command
TAJAG	The Assistant Judge Advocate General
TJAG	The Judge Advocate General
TJAGSA	The Judge Advocate General's School, U.S. Army
Tm	Team
Tng	Training
Trnsfd	Transferred
Univ	University
USA	U.S. Army
USALSA	U.S. Army Legal Services Agency
USAREUR	U.S. Army, Europe
USARSO	U.S. Army, South, Panama
USARV	U.S. Army, Vietnam
USATDS	U.S. Army Trial Defense Service
USMA	U.S. Military Academy, West Point, NY
USN	U.S. Navy

Andrews, Howard R. (1942–1970). BS (1965), Ga Tech; JD (1968), Univ of Ala. Enl, 101st Abn Div, Vietnam (1969). Commd JAGC (1970). JA, 25th Inf Div, Vietnam (1970). Died in Vietnam (1970). Participation in Vietnam.

Babbitt, Bruce C. (1920–1999). BA (1941) & LLB (1947), Univ of Mont. Inf Off, 32d Inf Div w/duty Philippines & Pacific Theatre (1942–45). Commd JAGC (1949). Mil Affrs Br, JAGO (1949–50). JA, 2d Inf Div, Ft Lewis (1950). JA, 3d Inf Div, Ft Benning (1957–58). SJA, 8th Inf Div, USAREUR (1959–61). Ch, GAD (1962–64). Exec Off, OTJAG (1966–68). SJA, MACV (1969–70). AJAG for Civ Law (1970–73). Retd, Brig Gen (1973). Participation in Vietnam.

Berry, J. Stevens (1938–). BA (1960), Stanford Univ; JD (1965), Northwestern Univ. Inf Off, Ft Leonard Wood (1960–61). Commd JAGC (1968). Ch DC, II Field Force, Vietnam (1968–69). REFRAD (1969). Participation in Vietnam.

Corrigan, Dennis M. (1940–). BA (1962), Fordham Univ; JD (1965), Rutgers Univ; MS (1978), C&GSC. Commd JAGC (1966). JA, USA Tng Ctr, Ft Ord (1967–69). JA, USA Spt Troops, U.S. Theater Army SUPCOM, USAREUR (1969–70). SJA, 1st Inf Div (Fwd), USAREUR (1970–72). JA, USARV, & MJ, USA Trial Judiciary, Vietnam (1972–73). S&F, TJAGSA (1974–77). SJA, 1st Inf Div (Fwd), USAREUR (1978–81). Lgl Adv, CJCS (1981–1985). SJA, 21st SUPCOM, USAREUR (1986–90). MJ, ACMR (1990–91). Ch, PP&TO, OTJAG (1991–93). Mil Asst, OGC, DoD (1993–95). Retd, Col (1995). Participation in Vietnam.

Crowley, Leonard G. (1933–). LLB (1957), Boston Coll; LLM (1971), Geo Wash Univ. Enl, Ft Buchanan, P.R. (1957–58). Commd JAGC (1958). Lgl Assistance Div, OTJAG (1960–62). JA, USA Antilles Comd, USARSO, Ft Brooke, P.R. (1962–66). JA, Fourth USA, Ft Sam Houston (1967–69). Ch, Foreign Claims Div, USARV (1969–70). USA Procurement Agcy, USARV (1971–72). OGC, Army & Air Force Exchange Svc, USAREUR (1972–75). DSJA, USA SUPCOM Hawaii, Ft Shafter (1975–77). Retd, Lt Col (1977). Participation in Vietnam.

Cuthbert, Thomas R. (1938–). BS (1961), USMA; MS (1964), Princeton Univ; JD (1967), Harvard Univ; LLM (1971), Northwestern Univ. Eng Off w/duty Korea (1961–63). Trnsfd to JAGC (1967). Patent Atty, OTJAG (1967–69). DSJA, 101st Abn Div, Vietnam (1969–70). OIC (Nuremberg) & DSJA, 1st Arm Div, USAREUR (1971–74). SJA, USA Tng Ctr, Ft Leonard Wood (1974–76). Ch, Mil Pers Law Br,

OTJAG (1977–81). Dir, Legislation & Lgl Policy, DoD (1982–86). SJA, VII Corps, USAREUR (1986–89). Ch, USATDS (1989–91). AJAG for Mil Law & Opns (1991–93). Cdr, USALSA & Ch Judge, ACCA (1993–95). Retd, Brig Gen (1996). Participation in Vietnam.

Deline, Donald A. (1943–). BA (1965), JD (1968) & MA (1968), Univ of Miss. Commd JAGC (1968). JA, Tooele Army Depot (1968–69). JA, USARV (1969–70). JA, USAREUR (1970–74). OCLL (1975–78). SJA, 101st Abn Div (1978–81). SJA, 9th Inf Div, Ft Lewis (1982–85). Lit Div, OTJAG (1985–87). SJA, V Corps, USAREUR (1988–90). Legislative Cnsl to Secretary of Def, DoD (1990–93). Retd, Col (1993). General Cnsl, Senate Armed Services Committee (1993–96). Participation in Vietnam.

Dommer, Paul P. (1937–1975). BA (1959), Canisius Col; LLB (1962) & LLM (1964), Georgetown Law Ctr. Commd JAGC (1967). JA, USA Air Def Ctr, Ft Bliss (1967–69). JA, OJA, USAREUR (1969–72). JA, MACV (1972–73). Intl Law Div, OTJAG (1973–75). Lgl Adv, Ofc of JCS (1975). Died on active duty (1975). Participation in Vietnam; a principal author of *Law at War*.

Douglass, John J. (1922–). BA (1943), Univ of Nebr; JD (1952) Univ of Mich.; LLM (1973), Univ of Va. Inf Off w/duty American Theatre (1944–46). Commd JAGC (1953). JA, FECOM, Japan & Korea (1953–54). Lit Div, OTJAG (1959–62). Exec Off, OJA, USAREUR (1963–66). SJA, USA Garrison, Ft Riley (1966–68). SJA, USARV (1968–69). MJ, USA Trial Judiciary (1969–70). Cmdt, TJAGSA (1970–74). Retd, Col (1974). Participation in Vietnam.

Downes, Michael M. (1935–). BA (1957) & LLB (1959), Univ of Ga. Commd JAGC (1963). DSJA, 23d Inf Div (Americal), Vietnam (1969–70). SJA, 2d Inf Div (1976–77). Lgl Adv, DA IG (1978–81). SJA, XVIII Abn Corps, Ft Bragg (1981–1985). SJA, USA Sig Ctr, Ft Gordon (1985–88). MJ, USA Trial Judiciary w/duty Ft Bragg (1988–90). Retd, Col (1990). Participation in Vietnam, Urgent Fury.

Durbin, Paul J. (1917–). BA (1938) & LLB (1941), Univ of Ky. Inf Off, w/duty France & Germany (1943–45). Commd JAGC (1948). JA, X Corps, FECOM, & 3d Log Cmd (1950). SJA, 7th Inf Div, Korea (1950–51). SJA, 1st Armd Div, Ft Hood (1952–53). SJA, 4th Armd Div, Ft Hood (1954). SJA, 82d Abn Div, Ft Bragg (1954–56). SJA, 101st Abn Div, Ft Campbell (1956–59). SJA, MAAG, Vietnam (1959–61). DSJA, USA Pacific, Ft Shafter (1962–65). DSJA, Fifth USA, Chicago (1965–66). SJA, II Field Force, Vietnam (1966). MJ,

USA Trial Judiciary w/duty Vietnam (1966–67). Retd, Col (1968). Participation in Vietnam.

Eblen, George C. (1921–). BS (1942) & LLB (1948), Univ of Tenn. Enl & Inf Off w/duty France & Germany (1942–46). Commd JAGC (1949). SJA, MAAG, Vietnam, & MACV (1961–62). SJA, USA Missile Cmd, Redstone Arsenal (1963–66). Retd, Lt Col (1966). Participation in Vietnam.

Felder, Ned E. (1937–). BA (1959) & LLB (1961), S.C. St Coll. Finance Off, Korea & Ft Totten (1961–63). Commd JAGC (1963). JA, 4th Inf Div, Ft Lewis & Vietnam (1963–66). JA, II Field Force, Vietnam (1966–68). JA, VII Corps, USAREUR (1969–72). DSJA, Berlin Bde (1972–73). MJ, USALSA (1973–81, 1984–88). SJA, USA Garrison, Ft Meade (1981–84). Retd, Col (1988). Participation in Vietnam.

Foreman, Leroy F. (1939–). BA (1961) & LLB (1963), Creighton Univ. Commd JAGC (1964). JA, 8th Inf Div, USAREUR (1964–67). JA, USA Inf Ctr, Ft Benning (1968–69). DSJA, XXIV Corps, Vietnam (1970–71). DSJA, USA Air Def Ctr, Ft Bliss (1971–72). SJA, Ft Hamilton (1973–75). PP&TO, OTJAG (1976–79). SJA, 2d Inf Div, Korea (1979–80). MJ, ACMR (1980–83). SJA, USA Arm Ctr, Ft Knox (1984–86). SJA, FORSCOM, Ft McPherson (1986–89). MJ, ACMR (1989–92). Retd, Col (1992). Participation in Vietnam.

Green, Herbert J. (1941–). BA (1963), Queens Coll; JD (1966), Univ of Tex. Commd JAGC (1966). JA, USA Garrison, Ft Sam Houston (1967–68). JA, II Field Force, Vietnam (1968–69). MJ, USA Trial Judiciary w/duty Ft Gordon, USAREUR, & Ft Lewis (1969–77). DSJA, USA Signal Ctr, Ft Gordon (1977–79). S&F, TJAGSA (1979–82). SJA, 1st Armd Div, USAREUR (1982–85). MJ, USA Trial Judiciary w/duty Ft Knox, USAREUR, & Ft Hood (1985–94). Retd, Col (1994). Participation in Vietnam.

Gray, Kenneth D. (1944–). BA (1966) W.Va. St Coll; JD (1969), Univ of W.Va. Commd JAGC (1969). DC, USA Tng Ctr, Ft Ord (1969–70). JA & DC, USA SUPCOM, USARV (1970–71). Asst Mil Affrs Off, First USA, Ft Meade (1971–72). PP&TO, OTJAG (1972–74). S&F, TJAGSA (1975–78). DSJA, 1st Arm Div, USAREUR (1978–80). SJA, 2d Armd Div, Ft Hood (1981–84). Ch, PP&TO, OTJAG (1984–87). SJA, III Corps, Ft Hood (1988–89). Sp Asst to TJAG (1989–90). Cdr, USALSA & Ch Judge, ACMR (1991–93). TAJAG (1993–97). Retd, Maj Gen (1997). Participation in Vietnam.

Hamlin, Guy A. (1923–1992). LLB (1950), Duke Univ. Enl & Inf Off w/duty France & Germany (1945–46). Commd JAGC (1950). JA, Okinawa Eng District, FECOM-Japan (1951–53). JA, Third USA, Ft McPherson (1953–57). JA, 7th Army, USAREUR (1958–62). SJA, 82d Abn Div, Ft Bragg & Dominican Republic (1963–66). JA, MACV, Vietnam (1966–67). SJA, 12th Support Bde, Ft Bragg (1967). Retd, Lt Col (1967). Participation in Power Pack, Vietnam.

Haughney, Edward W. (1917–). LLB (1949), St. Johns Univ; MS (1966), George Washington Univ. Arty Off, France & Germany (1942–47). Commd JAGC (1949). JA, FECOM (1950–53). S&F, TJAGSA (1954–58). Ch, Intl Affrs Br, OJA, USAREUR (1958–62). Asst Ch & Ch, Intl Affrs Div, OTJAG (1963–65). SJA, MACV (1966–67). Ch, Intl Affrs, OTJAG (1967–69). Lgl Adv, EUCOM (1969–72). Retd, Col (1972). Participation in Vietnam.

Hodson, Kenneth J. (1913–1995). BA (1935) & LLB (1937), Univ of Kans. Trnsfd to JAGD (1942). JA, Trinidad Base Sector & Base Cmd, Trinidad, W. Indies (1942–44). JA, Western Tactical Tng Cmd (Army Air Corps) (1944). JA, 52d Medium Port, Ft Hamilton & Le Havre, France (1944–45). Asst JA, Normandy Base Section, France (1945). SJA, Chanor Base Section, France (1946). Asst SJA, Exec Off, & SJA, Western Base Section, France (1946–47). Asst SJA, U.S. Constabulary, Paris, France (1947). Asst SJA & SJA, American Graves Registration Cmd (1947). Ch, Sp Projects Div & Asst to Board of Review No. 1 (1948–51). S&F, TJAGSA (1951–53). Asst SJA, Army Forces, Far East/Eighth USA (Rear) (1954–57). Ch, Mil Pers Div & Mil Jus Div & Exec Off, OTJAG (1958–62). AJAG for Mil Jus (1962–67). TJAG (1967–71). Retd & recalled (1971). Ch Judge, ACMR (1971–74). Retd, Maj Gen (1974).

Holdaway, Ronald M. (1934–). BA (1957) & LLB (1959), Univ of Wyo. Commd JAGC (1959). JA, 4th Inf Div, Ft Lewis (1960–63). JA, USA Hawaii (1963–66). S&F, TJAGSA (1967–69). SJA, 1st Cav Div, Vietnam (1969–70). Dep & Ch, GAD, USALSA (1970–75). Ch, PP&TO (1975–77). SJA, VII Corps, USAREUR (1978–80). Exec Off & AJAG for Civ Law (1980–83). JA, OJA, USAREUR (1983–87). Cdr, USALSA & Ch Judge, ACMR (1987–89). Retd, Brig Gen (1989). Participation in Vietnam.

Hunt, Dennis R. (1939–). JD (1964), Harvard Univ. Commd JAGC (1965). JA, 2d Inf Div, Korea (1965–66). Appellate Div, USA Judiciary (1966–69). MJ, USA Trial Judiciary, Vietnam (1969–70). MJ, USA Trial Judiciary w/duty USAREUR (1971–75). S&F, TJAGSA (1976–79). SJA, 24th Inf Div, Ft Stewart (1979–82). Cmd

Lgl Cnsl, USA Rcrtg Cmd (1982–84). Lgl Adv, DA IG (1985–87). Professor of Law, USMA (1987–98). Retd, Brig Gen (1998). Participation in Vietnam.

Kent, Irvin M. (1920–). BA (1940), Syracuse Univ; LLB (1947), Harvard Univ. Inf Off w/duty France & Germany (1943–45). Prosecution Staff, Nuremberg War Crimes Trials (1947). Commd JAGC (1948). JA, 1st Inf Div, EUCOM (1948–51). GAD, OTJAG (1951–54). SJA, First USA, Governors Island, N.Y. (1956–58). JA, 3d Log Cmd, USAREUR (1958–63). JA, USA Combat Development Cmd, Fts Gordon & Belvoir (1963–66). SJA, USA Air Def Cmd, Ent AFB, Colo. (1966–68). SJA, II Field Force & JA, MACV (1968–69). MJ, USA Trial Judiciary w/duty Ft Carson (1969–71). Retd, Col (1971). Participation in Vietnam.

Kulish, Jon N. (1938–). BA (1960), Univ of Santa Clara; JD (1967), Georgetown Univ; LLM (1976), George Washington Univ. Arm Off w/duty USAREUR (1960–64). Commd JAGC (1968). DSJA, II Field Force, Vietnam (1968–69). JA, Contract Appeals Div, USALSA (1971–75, 1976–80). Retd, Lt Col (1980). Participation in Vietnam.

Lamberth, Royce C. (1943–). BA (1965) & JD (1967), Univ of Tex. Enl, USA (1967). Commd JAGC (1968). JA, XVIII Abn Corps (1968–69). JA & DC, 1st Cav Div & Saigon SUPCOM, Vietnam (1969–70). Lit Div, OTJAG (1970–74). REFRAD (1974). Judge, U.S. District Court for District of Columbia (1987–present). Participation in Vietnam.

McNamee, Alfred A. (1931–). BA (1958), Univ of Fla.; LLB (1961), Wake Forest Univ. Enl & Inf Off w/duty USAREUR, Ft Benning, & Ft Bragg (1949–63). Trnsfd to JAGC (1962). JA, 101st Abn Div, Ft Campbell (1963–64). SJA, USA SUPCOM, Vietnam (1964–65). S&F, TJAGSA (1965–67). SJA, 5th Inf Div, Ft Carson (1967–68). DSJA & SJA, USA Arm Ctr, Ft Knox (1968–71). S&F, C&GSC, Ft Leavenworth (1972–75). Lgl Adv, Allied Forces Europe, South, Italy (1975–78). Retd, Col (1978). Participation in Vietnam.

Miller, Hubert E. (1918–). LLB (1941), Albany Law Sch; MA (1964), George Washington Univ. Inf Off w/duty France & Germany (1943–45) & Korea (1950–52). Trnsfd to JAGC (1953). S&F, TJAGSA (1956–57). DSJA, 101st Abn Div, Ft Campbell (1957–59). SJA, 1st Cav Div, Korea (1959–60). Mil Jus Br, OTJAG (1960–63). DSJA, USA Pacific, Hawaii (1964–66). SJA, 1st Log Cmd, Vietnam (1966–67). MJ, USA Judiciary, OTJAG (1967–68). S&F, War Coll

(1971–72). SJA, USA Air Def Cmd, Ent AFB (1972–74). SJA, USA Air Def Ctr, Ft Bliss (1974–75). Retd, Col (1975). Participation in Vietnam.

Miranda, Ralph G. (1938–). BA (1959), Tex. West Coll; LLB (1962), Univ of San Francisco. Commd JAGC (1964). JA, USA Pacific, Okinawa, Japan (1964–65). JA, USA Garrison, Ft Ord (1966–67). JA, VII Corps, USAREUR (1967–70). JA, USARV (1971–72). DSJA, USA Arty Ctr, Ft Sill (1972–73). Trnsfd to USAR (1973). JA, 22d JAG Det, Austin, Tex. (1977–87). Retd, Lt Col (1987).

Moushegian, Vahan, Jr. (1942–). BA (1965), Vanderbilt; LLB (1968), Univ of Va. Trnsfd to JAGC (1972). JA, USARV/MACV (1972–73). JA, V Corps & OJA, USAREUR (1973–76). Adm Law Div, OTJAG (1977–82). DSJA, 1st Inf Div (Mech) (1983–86). Adm Law Div, OTJAG (1986–88). SJA, 24th Inf Div (1988–91). Lgl Adv, USA Surgeon General (1991–94). SJA, First USA, Ft Meade (1994–95). Retd, Col (1995). Participation in Vietnam, deployed to Florida during Hurricane Andrew relief efforts (1992).

Myers, William G. (1924–). BS (1944), Southwest La. Institute (1944); MA (1948), Univ of Ark.; JD (1955), Univ of Mich. Enl & Off, USN (1943–49). Commd JAGC (1956). JA, USAREUR (1956–59). JA, MACV (1963–64). SJA, 4th Log Cmd, Ft Lee (1965–67). Retd, Lt Col (1970). Participation in Vietnam.

Prugh, George S. (1920–). BA (1941), Univ of Calif.–Berkeley; LLB (1948), Hastings Coll, Univ of Calif.; MA (1963), George Washington Univ. Enl, Calif. NG & Coast Art Off w/duty Philippines & Pacific Theatre (1939–44). Commd JAGC (1947). Mil Jus, Claims & Lit Divs, OTJAG (1949–50). JA, Wetzlar Mil Post, USAREUR (1950–51). Exec Off & SJA, Rhine Mil Post, USAREUR (1951–53). Board of Review & Mil Jus Div, OTJAG (1953–56). DSJA, Eighth USA (1957–58). DSJA & Asst Exec Reserve Affrs, Sixth USA, Presidio of San Francisco (1958–61). Ch, Career Mgmt Div & Exec Off, OTJAG (1962–64). SJA, MACV (1964–66). Lgl Adv, EUCOM w/duty France & Germany (1966–69). JA, OJA, USAREUR (1969–71). TJAG (1971–75). Retd, Maj Gen (1975). Participation in Vietnam.

Radosh, Burnett H. (1935–). BA (1953), Univ of Chicago; LLB (1956), N.Y. Univ; LLM (1960), Georgetown Univ. Enl w/duty Ft Benning (1958–59). Commd JAGC (1959). DAD, OTJAG (1959–61). CJA, 4th Log Cmd & 1st Log Cmd, France (1961–62). 4th Log Cmd, France (1962–63). 3d Log Cmd, France (1963–64). DSJA, 82d Abn

Div, Ft Bragg & Dominican Republic (1965–66). JA, 1st Log Cmd, Vietnam (1966–67). CAD, OTJAG (1967–70). SJA, 25th Inf Div, Vietnam (1970–71). CAD, USALSA (1971–74). Ch, Mil Pers Br, Lit Div, OTJAG (1974–75). Adm Judge, Armed Svc Board Contract Appeals (1975–78). SJA, USA Tng Ctr, Ft Dix (1978–79). SJA, DA Materiel Development & Readiness Cmd (1979–80). Retd, Col (1980). Participation in Power Pack, Vietnam.

Robinson, George R. (1925–1989). LLB (1950), Univ of Okla. Enl, USN w/duty Atlantic (1943–45) & Korea (1948–50). Commd JAGC (1950). JA, 82d Abn Div, Ft Bragg (1959–63). JA, 101st Abn Div, Ft Campbell (1963–64). JA, MACV (1964–65). JA, DSJA & SJA, USA Arty Ctr, Ft Sill (1965–68). MJ, USA Trial Judiciary w/duty Ft Sill & Ft Bragg (1968–72). SJA, USA Arty Ctr, Ft Sill (1972–73). Retd, Col (1973). Participation in Vietnam.

Scanlon, Jerome W., Jr. (1940–). BA (1961), St. Bonaventure Univ; JD (1964), Fordham Univ. Arty Off w/duty USAREUR (1966–69) Trnsfd to JAGC (1969). JA, USA Tng Ctr, Ft Dix (1969–1972). Lgl Off, Def Attaché Ofc w/duty Saigon, Vietnam (1973–74). DSJA, USA Arty Ctr, Ft Sill (1974–77). S&F, USMA (1977–81). SJA, USA Garrison, Ft Sam Houston (1981–85). Retd, Lt Col (1985). Participation in Vietnam.

Sherwood, John T., Jr. (1935–1995). BS (1960) & JD (1962), American Univ; LLM (1975), Univ of Mich. Commd JAGC (1963). JA, 82d Abn Div, Ft Bragg (1963–65). JA, MACV (1965–66). S&F, USMA (1966–70). OIC (Nuremberg), VII Corps, USAREUR (1970–73). DSJA, USMA (1977–80). DSJA, Sixth USA, Presidio of San Francisco (1980–83). SJA, 19th SUPCOM, Korea (1983–85). SJA, Third USA, Ft McPherson (1985–86). Retd, Col (1986). Participation in Vietnam.

Solf, Waldemar A. (1913–1987). LLB (1937), Univ of Chicago. Arty Off (1942–46) w/duty France & Germany. Trnsfd to JAGD (1946). MJ, USA Trial Judiciary w/duty Korea & Ft Meade (1959–62). SJA, Eighth USA, Korea & U.S. Strat Cmd (1962–65). Ch, Mil Jus Div, OTJAG (1966–68). Retd, Col (1968). DA Civilian, Intl Affrs Div, OTJAG (1970–71). Ch, Intl Affrs Div, OTJAG (1971–77). Sp Asst to TJAG (1977–79). Delegate, Diplomatic Conference on the Reaffirmation and Development of Humanitarian Law in Armed Conflict (1977 Protocols to Geneva Conventions) (1975–77). Retd, DA Civilian (1979).

Suter, William K. (1937–). AB (1959), Trinity Univ; LLB (1962), Tulane Univ. Commd JAGC (1962). JA, USA Alaska (1963–66). S&F, TJAGSA (1967–70). Asst SJA, USA SUPCOM, Thailand (1970). DSJA, USARV (1971). OTJAG (1971–74). SJA, 101st Abn Div, Ft Campbell (1975–77). Ch, PP&TO, OTJAG (1977–79). Cmdt, TJAGSA (1981–84). Cdr, USALSA & Ch Judge, ACMR (1984–85). TAJAG (1985–1989). Acting TJAG (1989–91). Retired, Maj Gen (1991). Clerk of Court, U.S. Supreme Court. Participation in Vietnam.

Taylor, Arthur H. (1930–). AA & LLB (1954), Boston Univ. Trnsfd to JAGC (1960). JA, USA Tng Ctr, Ft Dix (1960–62). JA, USA Support Grp, Vietnam (1962–63). JA, XVIII Abn Corps w/duty Ft Bragg & Dominican Republic (1964–66). SJA, JFKSWC, Ft Bragg (1967–68). JA, US Air Def Cmd, Ent AFB (1968–69). JA, Eighth USA, Korea, & SJA, Korea SUPCOM (1971–72). Exec Reserve Affrs, FORSCOM, Ft McPherson (1972–74). Retd, Lt Col (1974). Participation in Vietnam, Power Pack.

Tenhet, Joseph N., Jr. (1924–). LLB (1949), Univ of Richmond; LLM (1950), Duke Univ. Inf Off w/duty France & Germany (1943–46). Commd JAGC (1953). JA, Mil Affrs Div, OTJAG (1953–55). JA, 23d Inf Div, USA Caribbean, Panama (1955–58). JA, Fourth USA, Ft Sam Houston (1959–62). JA, Eighth USA, Korea (1963–64). Mil Affrs Div, OTJAG (1964–69). SJA, 3d Inf Div, USAREUR (1969–70). SJA, V Corps, USAREUR (1970–71). SJA, USARV & MACV (1972–73). Ch, Adm Law Div, OTJAG (1973–75). AJAG for Mil Law (1975–78). Retd, Brig Gen (1978). Participation in Vietnam.

Weaver, Robert K. (1920–). BS (1943) & LLB (1947), Univ of S.Dak. Commd JAGC (1949). JA, EUCOM (1950–53). S&F, TJAGSA (1954–58). Asst SJA, VII Corps, USAREUR (1958–61). S&F, USMA (1961–65). SJA, MAAG, Taiwan (1965–67). Ch, Lit Div, OTJAG (1967–70). SJA, MACV (1970–71). Ch, Procurement Law Div, OTJAG (1971–74). Retd, Col (1974). Participation in Vietnam.

Westerman, George F. (1916–1985). BS (1939) & LLB (1947), Univ of Wis. Signal Off w/duty France & Germany (1941–45). Commd JAGC (1947). Asst SJA, MDW (1947–50). JA, Eighth USA & Japan Log Cmd w/duty Korea (1950–52). Ch, Patents Div, OTJAG (1952–56). Patent Adv, U.S. Mission to NATO, Paris, France (1957–60). Ch, Patents Div, OTJAG (1961–62). SJA, MACV (1962–63). Ch, Mil Affrs Div & Ch, Intl Affrs Div, OTJAG (1963–67). MJ & Ch Judge, ACMR (1968–70). Retd, Col (1971). Participation in Vietnam.

White, Charles A., Jr. (1939–). BA (1961) & JD (1963), Coll Wm & Mary; MA (1968), Tufts Univ. Commd JAGC (1964). Asst SJA, 173d Abn Inf Bde w/duty Okinawa & Vietnam (1964–66). JA, Career Mgmt Div, OTJAG (1966–68). Intl Affrs Div, OTJAG (1968–69). Ch, Intl Affrs Div, OJA, USAREUR (1969–72). S&F, TJAGSA (1973–76). SJA, 1st Cav Div, Ft Hood (1976–79). SJA, 21st SUPCOM (1980–83). Lgl Cnsl, Intelligence Opns, DoD (1983–84). Retd, Col (1984). Participation in Vietnam.

Williams, Lawrence H. (1922–1999). BS (1947), Univ of Minn.; JD (1948), Univ of Colo. Aviation Off w/duty No. Africa, France, & Germany (1942–46). Commd JAGC (1948). Mil Affrs Div, OTJAG (1948–52). S&F, TJAGSA (1952–53). JA, USA Carribean, Panama (1953–56). Asst Lgl Adv, Ofc Dep Ch Staff Logistics, Washington, D.C. (1956–57). Mil Affrs Div, OTJAG (1957–61). SJA & Asst Ch Staff (G–1), 3d Armd Div, USAREUR (1961–64). Ch, Mil Affrs Div, OTJAG (1964–66). SJA, III Corps, Ft Hood (1967–69). SJA, MACV (1969–70). Ch, Mil Affrs Div, OTJAG (1970–71). AJAG for Mil Law (1971–75). TAJAG (1975–79). Retd, Maj Gen (1979). Participation in Vietnam.

Index

156

www.ingramcontent.com/pod-product-compliance
Lightning Source LLC
Chambersburg PA
CBHW021403090426
42742CB00009B/987